Build Your N Mastery of PDO with PHP & Java:

A Practical Guide to Secure Database Programming on Linux and Windows

Written by, Lynne Kolestar

Table of Contents

Introduction

In today's world of web development and software engineering, interacting with databases is a fundamental skill for any developer, as well as for professionals involved in software installation and maintenance. Whether you're building a dynamic website, an enterprise-level application, or a simple CRUD app, databases are at the heart of most modern applications. Over the years, developers have used various methods to connect to and manage databases, but PDO (PHP Data Objects) has emerged as one of the most reliable, secure, and flexible approaches for working with databases in both PHP and Java.

This book is designed to help you master PDO and unlock its full potential for creating, installing, and maintaining secure, efficient, and cross-platform database-driven applications. While PHP has long been a dominant language for server-side web development, Java is also a powerful option, especially for larger, scalable applications.

One of PDO's key advantages is its ability to provide a consistent, secure method for interacting with databases, regardless of the programming language or platform. PDO is widely regarded as a universal and secure solution for communication between server and database, supported across various programming environments, including PHP, Java, C++, Python, and more. Whether you're building dynamic web applications with PHP, developing large-scale enterprise systems with Java, or working with other supported languages, PDO enables seamless connectivity to MySQL and other databases, enhancing productivity, scalability, and maintainability.

Why this book?

In the ever-evolving world of web development, securely interacting with databases is crucial for any developer. This book is designed to teach you how to master PDO (PHP Data Objects) for database operations, offering a secure, flexible, and efficient way to interact with databases in both PHP and Java. Whether you're a beginner or an experienced developer, you'll gain the skills necessary to create, maintain, and troubleshoot database-driven applications with PDO.

PDO is a powerful tool that allows you to work seamlessly across platforms and languages. In this guide, we dive into how PDO can be used in both PHP for web applications and Java for large-scale enterprise systems. You'll see how PDO offers a consistent interface regardless of language, helping you work with databases like MySQL, PostgreSQL, SQLite, and others, without having to rewrite large parts of your codebase. PDO's use of prepared statements ensures secure database interactions, protecting against SQL injection vulnerabilities, which makes it a much safer alternative to older methods like MySQLi or JDBC.

By the end of this book, you'll not only be proficient in using PDO for both PHP and Java but also understand how to set up your development environment, manage database connections, perform CRUD operations, handle transactions, and more. You will have mastered the art of building scalable, secure, and maintainable database-driven applications.

Why PDO over MySQLi or JDBC?

PDO stands out as the most secure and flexible solution for database interactions. One of the major advantages of PDO is its built-in protection against SQL injection, using prepared statements to safeguard your application from malicious database queries. Unlike MySQLi or JDBC, PDO is database-agnostic, allowing you to switch between different databases like MySQL, PostgreSQL, SQLite, and others without making substantial changes to your codebase. This flexibility makes PDO a future-proof choice for developers working on both web applications and enterprise-level systems.

In this book, we'll guide you through the installation and configuration of PDO for both PHP and Java, across different operating systems (Linux and Windows). We'll then explore how to use PDO for secure and efficient database connections, performing operations like CRUD, managing transactions, and handling errors. By mastering PDO, you'll be ready to build robust applications that can scale and adapt to changing technologies and databases.

Who is This Book For?

This book is designed for developers, system administrators, and IT professionals at any stage of their career, whether you're just starting out or looking to expand your expertise. It's written in a clear, easy-to-follow structure, making it accessible to anyone seeking to grasp key concepts, rules, and best practices. Along the way, I've included some of my own tips and tricks to simplify your journey with MySQL and PDO.

Beginners in PHP or Java Who Are New to PDO

If you're new to PHP or Java and just getting started with database-driven applications, this book is an ideal starting point. We'll guide you through the basics of using PDO for secure database connections in both languages, without assuming any prior knowledge or experience with PDO or database programming. You'll learn key concepts like prepared statements, CRUD operations, transactions, and error handling through clear, easy-to-follow examples. By the end of the book, you'll have a solid foundation in MySQL and PDO, equipping you to build secure, efficient, and scalable applications.

Intermediate Developers Wanting to Improve Security or Switch from MySQLi to PDO

For developers who already have experience with PHP or Java but are looking to improve their database security practices or move from MySQLi (in PHP) or JDBC (in Java) to PDO, this book will provide the perfect opportunity. You'll learn how PDO offers built-in protection against SQL injection, a critical vulnerability in many applications. The book walks you through the benefits of switching to PDO, including how it simplifies working with multiple database systems (such as MySQL, PostgreSQL, SQLite, and more) and ensures that your applications are more secure and flexible. Whether you're working on small projects or large-scale systems, PDO will help you streamline your database interactions.

Linux and Windows Users Looking to Set Up a Development Environment with Secure Database Interactions

Whether you're using a Linux (Debian/Ubuntu) or Windows system, this book will help you set up a local development environment tailored to your platform of choice. We'll show you how to install PDO, configure database connections, and ensure your development environment is secure and ready for building robust applications. You'll also find guidance on using popular development stacks like XAMPP, MAMP, or LAMP, and how to integrate JDBC drivers for Java users. If you're looking to ensure that your database interactions are secure and properly configured on your chosen platform, this book provides a comprehensive guide for both beginners and experienced users.

Chapter 1: PDO vs. MySQLi

When developing PHP applications that interact with MySQL databases, developers often choose between two primary database access libraries: PDO (PHP Data Objects) and MySQLi (MySQL Improved). Both offer methods for connecting to and interacting with MySQL databases, but they differ in several key aspects, including flexibility, security, and syntax. In this section, we'll compare the two and highlight the reasons why PDO is often considered the better choice.

Understanding the Differences: PDO vs. MySQLi

Database Support:

PDO: PDO is a database abstraction layer that supports not just MySQL but also multiple other database systems, such as PostgreSQL, SQLite, and MS SQL Server. This makes it a more flexible and portable option for developers who may need to switch to or work with different databases in the future.

MySQLi: MySQLi, as the name implies, is specifically designed for MySQL databases. It does not support other databases, so it is less flexible than PDO.

Winner: PDO — PDO's ability to connect to multiple databases makes it more versatile for projects that may scale beyond MySQL.

Object-Oriented vs. Procedural:

PDO: PDO is strictly object-oriented, meaning that you interact with the database using objects and methods. This can help to organize your code and improve maintainability, especially in larger applications.

MySQLi: MySQLi supports both object-oriented and procedural programming styles. This flexibility can be helpful for developers who prefer a procedural approach, especially in smaller scripts or for those migrating from procedural codebases.

Winner: Tie — The choice between object-oriented and procedural style depends on the developer's preference and the project's requirements. However, in modern PHP development, object-oriented programming (OOP) is generally preferred, making PDO more attractive in such cases.

Prepared Statements:

PDO: PDO supports prepared statements natively, which is a key feature for writing secure and efficient database queries. Prepared statements allow you to separate SQL logic from user input, making it much harder for attackers to exploit your queries through SQL injection.

MySQLi: MySQLi also supports prepared statements, but the syntax for using them is more complex and requires more code.

Winner: PDO – PDO's support for prepared statements is simpler and more consistent across different databases, improving both security and ease of use.

Fetching Data:

PDO: PDO offers various methods for fetching data from the database, such as fetch(), fetchAll(), and fetchColumn(). You can fetch rows as an associative array, a numeric array, or both, giving you flexibility in how you handle the result set.

MySQLi: MySQLi also provides several methods for fetching data, such as fetch_assoc(), fetch_row(), and fetch_object(). While similar to PDO, the methods are somewhat less flexible when compared to PDO's options.

Winner: PDO – PDO provides more options and flexibility for fetching data from the database.

Binding Parameters:

PDO: PDO allows you to bind parameters by reference, which can make it more efficient when working with variables in complex queries. This binding ensures that the values are sanitized and securely handled before executing the query.

MySQLi: MySQLi also supports parameter binding but only with the procedural style. Binding is slightly more verbose and harder to work with when using the object-oriented approach.

Winner: PDO – PDO's parameter binding is more flexible and efficient, especially when dealing with object-oriented code.

Error Handling:

PDO: PDO uses exceptions for error handling, which means you can use try-catch blocks to catch and handle errors gracefully. This allows for cleaner code and better debugging.

MySQLi: MySQLi offers error handling in both the procedural and object-oriented styles, but it relies on manual checks for errors (using functions like mysqli_error() or mysqli_errno()). This can lead to more error-prone code, especially in larger applications.

Winner: PDO – PDO's use of exceptions makes error handling more intuitive and less error-prone than MySQLi's manual error checks.

Why PDO is Better

Database Abstraction and Flexibility

One of the main advantages of using PDO is its database abstraction. While MySQLi is specifically designed for MySQL databases, PDO can interact with many different types of databases, such as PostgreSQL, SQLite, and MSSQL. This means that if you start a project with MySQL but later decide to migrate to another database, you can typically do so with minimal changes to your PHP code by adjusting just the connection string.

Why it Matters

Using PDO enhances your application's portability and future-proofing. If you're working on a project that may need to support multiple databases in the future or if you want the flexibility to switch databases with minimal effort, PDO is the ideal choice.

Prepared Statements and SQL Injection Protection

One of the key reasons PDO is preferred is its robust protection against SQL injection attacks. PDO uses prepared statements, which separate query logic from user input, preventing malicious users from injecting harmful SQL code into your queries—a common vulnerability in many web applications. For instance, any application handling sensitive data, such as financial or medical records, would prioritize secure practices like those provided by PDO to ensure data integrity. Shouldn't you do the same for your application?

Here's how PDO's prepared statements help prevent SQL injection:

```
$sql = "SELECT * FROM users WHERE email = :email";
$stmt = $pdo->prepare($sql);
$stmt->bindParam(':email', $email);
$stmt->execute();
```

In the example above, even if a user enters malicious input (e.g., ' OR 1=1;--), PDO will treat it as a string, not executable SQL, thus protecting your application from SQL injection attacks.

Why it Matters

Security: Prepared statements in PDO are safer and less error-prone than building SQL queries manually. They automatically handle escaping and sanitizing user input, significantly reducing the risk of SQL injection.

Error Handling and Debugging

PDO uses exceptions for error handling, meaning that when an error occurs, PDO will throw an exception that can be caught using try-catch blocks. This makes error handling much cleaner and easier to manage than MySQLi, which requires manual error checks.

Example of PDO error handling:

```
try {
    $pdo = new PDO($dsn, $user, $password);
```

```
    $pdo->setAttribute(PDO::ATTR_ERRMODE,
PDO::ERRMODE_EXCEPTION);

} catch (PDOException $e) {
    echo "Error: " . $e->getMessage();
}
```

Using exceptions allows for better error management, cleaner code, and more helpful debugging. Developers can catch errors and handle them in a structured way, instead of manually checking error codes and handling them ad-hoc.

Support for Transactions

PDO provides better support for transactions, making it easy to group multiple SQL queries into a single transaction. If one query fails, you can roll back the entire transaction, ensuring that no partial data is saved to the database.

Example of a PDO transaction:

```
try {
    $pdo->beginTransaction();

    // Execute your SQL queries here...

    $pdo->commit();
    // Commit the transaction if all queries are successful

} catch (Exception $e) {
    $pdo->rollBack(); // Rollback the transaction in case of an error
    echo "Failed: " . $e->getMessage();
}
```

Transactions ensure data integrity and help prevent partial

updates to the database. This is especially important in applications that require multiple related queries to be executed as a group.

Why PDO is the Better Choice

PDO is more flexible as it supports multiple database systems, not just MySQL.

PDO is more future-proof, offering greater flexibility and support for multiple database systems, while MySQLi is limited to MySQL databases.

Security: PDO provides better security by using prepared statements to prevent SQL injection attacks.

Error handling is more intuitive with PDO's use of exceptions.

Transactions in PDO are easier to work with, helping maintain data integrity.

While MySQLi is still a good option for MySQL-specific projects, PDO is the preferred choice for modern, secure, and maintainable PHP applications. Its flexibility, security features, and ease of use make it the superior option for database interactions.

Chapter 2: Setting Up Your Development Environment

Before diving into the world of PDO and secure database programming, it's essential to establish a solid development environment. Whether you are using PHP or Java, having your setup properly configured will allow you to focus on writing code instead of troubleshooting environment issues. In this chapter, we'll guide you through setting up a development environment for both PHP and Java on Linux and Windows platforms, covering the necessary tools and software to get you up and running with PDO.

For PHP, you'll need a web server, PHP itself, and a database management system like MySQL or MariaDB for Debian/Ubuntu Linux systems. One of the easiest ways to get started is by using a software stack like XAMPP (cross-platform), MAMP (for macOS), or LAMP (for Linux). These all-in-one packages bundle Apache, MySQL, and PHP together in a single installation, making the setup process quick and easy. Alternatively, you can manually install each component, giving you more control over the configuration.

Whichever method you choose, we'll walk you through the installation and configuration of these tools, including how to configure the PHP PDO extension. This extension is often included by default, but may need to be enabled in your php.ini file for full functionality.

For Java, setting up the environment involves installing the Java Development Kit (JDK) and configuring JDBC drivers for database connectivity. Java developers often use popular Integrated Development Environments (IDEs) such as Eclipse, IntelliJ IDEA, or NetBeans, which simplify managing dependencies and configuring database connections. To replicate PDO-like functionality in Java, you'll need to install the appropriate JDBC driver for your database system, such as MySQL Connector/J for MySQL databases. We'll guide you through the installation of the JDK, JDBC drivers, and setting up the necessary IDE tools. Once configured, you'll be able to use JDBC to connect to your database and perform operations similar to PDO's prepared statements.

Whether you're using PHP or Java, it's crucial to ensure that your database system (MySQL, PostgreSQL, SQLite, etc.) is installed and accessible from your development environment. In this chapter, we'll walk you through installing and configuring your database, establishing your first database connection, and verifying that everything works smoothly. With our step-by-step instructions, you'll have your environment set up correctly in no time, allowing you to focus on mastering PDO to its full potential.

Debian/Ubuntu Linux (X11 and CLI)

Install MariaDB/MySQL, PHP, and Apache/Nginx

Setting up a development environment on Debian or Ubuntu Linux for PHP, Java, and database management requires some key installations and configurations. This section will walk you through step-by-step instructions for both of Linux's graphical (X11) and command-line interface (CLI) environments, covering the installation of MariaDB, PHP, Apache/Nginx, and Java (JDK). Additionally, we'll guide you through setting up phpMyAdmin for database management and configuring a Java environment similar to PDO with JDBC.

Installing MariaDB/MySQL, PHP, and Apache/Nginx (CLI and X11)

To get started, you'll need to install the following core components on your Debian/Ubuntu system:

MariaDB (a drop-in replacement for MySQL)
PHP (with PDO extension)
Apache or **Nginx** (web servers)

Step-by-Step Installation (CLI)
Login with your terminal (CLI) and update your package lists to ensure you're installing the latest versions:

Update Package Lists:
sudo apt update

sudo apt upgrade

Install MariaDB:
sudo apt install mariadb-server

Once installed, secure your MariaDB/MySQL installation:
sudo mysql_secure_installation

You will be prompted to configure some security settings, such as setting up a root password and removing insecure default settings.

Follow the prompts to complete the setup:

Set a strong root password for the MariaDB administrator account.

Decide whether to remove test databases and anonymous user accounts for additional security.

Create a MySQL User for Website Access:

After securing MariaDB, it's essential to create a dedicated database user for your website to access the database securely.

First, log in to the MariaDB shell using the mysql command:
sudo mysql -u root -p

You will be prompted for the root password you set earlier.

Create the Database and User:

Inside the MariaDB shell, create a new database and a user that will have access to it.

Replace YourDatabaseName, YourUserName, and YourPassword with your desired values:

CREATE DATABASE YourDatabaseName;

CREATE USER 'YourUserName'@'localhost' IDENTIFIED BY 'YourPassword';

Grant Privileges to the New User:

After creating the user, grant it the necessary permissions to access the newly created database. This allows the user to perform actions like SELECT, INSERT, UPDATE, DELETE, etc., on the database.

To grant all privileges on YourDatabaseName database to the YourUserName on localhost:

GRANT ALL PRIVILEGES ON YourDatabaseName.* TO 'YourUserName'@'localhost';

To grant privileges to the user 'YourUserName' on a specific IP range like 192.168.1.*, you can use the following syntax:

GRANT ALL PRIVILEGES ON YourDatabaseName.* TO 'YourUserName'@'192.168.1.%';

Flush Privileges and Exit

To ensure that the changes take effect, run the following command:

FLUSH PRIVILEGES;

Then, exit the MariaDB shell:

EXIT;

Verify the Database Access
You can verify that the new user has the appropriate privileges by logging in as the newly created user:

mysql -u YourUserName -p

When prompted, enter the password you set for the user. **After logging in, you can check that the user has access to the database by running:**

SHOW DATABASES;

You should see the YourDatabaseName listed.

Install Apache or Nginx

Choose between Apache or Nginx as your web server.

Install Apache:

sudo apt install apache2

Alternatively, to install Nginx:

sudo apt install nginx

Install PHP along with the necessary extensions:

sudo apt install php php-mysqli php-pdo php-cli php-fpm

After installation, ensure the PHP pdo extension is enabled. You can check this by running:

php -m | grep pdo

If not enabled, you can enable it by editing the php.ini configuration file and restarting the service.

Install phpMyAdmin

phpMyAdmin is a web interface for managing your MariaDB/MySQL databases.

Install it by running:

sudo apt install phpmyadmin

Follow the prompts to configure phpMyAdmin with Apache/Nginx. During installation, select Apache or Nginx as the web server. After installation, you can access phpMyAdmin by navigating to http://localhost/phpmyadmin in your browser.

Installation (X11 Graphical Environment)

Install Necessary Packages Using GUI

Open Debian/Ubuntu Software or Synaptic Package Manager and search for and install the following packages:

MariaDB (or MySQL)
Apache or **Nginx**
PHP and the relevant PDO extensions
phpMyAdmin

Follow the prompts in the installation GUI to configure each tool as needed.

Configure the Web Server

Once the software is installed, open your browser and check if your web server (Apache/Nginx) is running by navigating to http://localhost. If the server is running correctly, you should see the default web page.

Create a test PHP file (a text file) named info.php and save it to the /var/www/html directory for Apache or to the /usr/share/nginx/html directory for Nginx:

Create info.php

```php
<?php

phpinfo();

?>
```

Save the text file in /var/www/html/info.php for the Apache web server.

Or

Save the text file in /usr/share/nginx/html/info.php for the Nginx web server.

Navigate to http://localhost/info.php in your browser. If PHP is correctly installed, you will see a page displaying PHP information.

Install Java, MariaDB/MySQL, and Apache/Nginx (CLI and X11)

Now that PHP and MariaDB/MySQL are installed, let's add Java (JDK) and configure MariaDB/MySQL with Java to create a PDO-like environment using JDBC.

Installing Java (JDK)

To install Java on your Debian-based system:

sudo apt install openjdk-11-jdk

Confirm the installation by running:

java -version

Configure Environment Variables

To ensure the JDK is accessible globally, you can set the environment variables.

Edit your ~/.bashrc or ~/.profile file:

nano ~/.bashrc

Add the following lines to the end:

```
export JAVA_HOME=/usr/lib/jvm/java-11-openjdk-amd64
export PATH=$PATH:$JAVA_HOME/bin
```

Save the file and apply the changes:

source ~/.bashrc

Installing JDBC Drivers for MariaDB

To use MariaDB with Java, you'll need to install the MariaDB JDBC driver.

Download the MariaDB JDBC Driver from the official website:

wget https://downloads.mariadb.com/Connectors/java/2.7.3/mariadb-java-client-2.7.3.jar

Move the downloaded .jar file to a directory like /usr/local/lib.

Configure JDBC with Apache/Nginx

In your Java code, use the MariaDB JDBC driver to establish a MySQL connection:

```java
import java.sql.*;

public class Main {
    public static void main(String[] args) {
        // Replace with your actual database credentials
        String url = "jdbc:mariadb://localhost:3306/YourDatabaseName";
        String user = "YourUserName";
        String password = "YourPassword";

        // JDBC variables for opening a connection
        try (Connection con = DriverManager.getConnection(url, user, password);

            Statement stmt = con.createStatement();
            ResultSet rs = stmt.executeQuery("SELECT * FROM table"))
{

            // Register the JDBC driver (optional in newer versions)
            // Class.forName("org.mariadb.jdbc.Driver");
            // Above not needed in modern versions

            // Extract data from the result set
            while (rs.next()) {
                // Example: printing the first column's value
                System.out.println(rs.getString(1));
            }

        } catch (SQLException e) {
            // Handle SQL exceptions
            System.out.println("An error occurred while connecting to the database or executing the query.");
            e.printStackTrace();
        }
    }
}
```

This sets up the JDBC connection using MariaDB, similar to how PDO works in PHP.

MS Windows Systems

To start building dynamic web applications or run Java-based database programs, it's crucial to have the correct software installed on your Windows system. This section will walk you through installing MariaDB/MySQL, PHP, Apache/Nginx, phpMyAdmin, and Java (JDK), and configuring them for use on your local development environment.

Installing MariaDB/MySQL, PHP, and Apache/Nginx on Windows

There are two ways to set up a local development environment on Windows: using an all-in-one software package like XAMPP, or installing each component manually for more control over your configuration.

Option 1: Using XAMPP (Easiest Way)

XAMPP is a free and open-source cross-platform web server solution stack package that includes Apache, MariaDB, PHP, and phpMyAdmin. It is ideal for those who want a quick setup for development.

Download XAMPP:

Go to the XAMPP website. Download the version that matches your operating system (Windows).

Install XAMPP:
Run the installer and follow the on-screen instructions. Choose the components to install (make sure to include Apache, MariaDB, and PHP).

Start the Services:
Open the XAMPP Control Panel. Start the Apache and MariaDB services by clicking the "Start" buttons next to them.

Access phpMyAdmin:
Open your browser and go to http://localhost/phpmyadmin.

This will open the phpMyAdmin interface where you can manage your databases.

Option 2: Manual Installation of MariaDB/MySQL, PHP, and Apache/Nginx

If you prefer to manually configure each component for more control over your setup, follow the steps below.

Install Apache (Web Server):
Download the Apache Lounge version of Apache HTTP Server for Windows. Extract the files to a directory of your choice

(e.g., C:\Apache24).

Open a command prompt as Administrator and navigate to the Apache directory.

Run the following command to install Apache as a service:

httpd.exe -k install

Start Apache:

httpd.exe -k start

Install MariaDB/MySQL:
Download the MariaDB installer from the official website. Run the installer and follow the instructions to install MariaDB on your system. After installation, MariaDB should automatically start as a service.

Install PHP:
Download the PHP Windows binaries from the PHP for Windows website. Extract the files to a folder (e.g., C:\php).

Edit the Apache configuration file (httpd.conf) to integrate PHP by adding the following lines at the end of the file:

LoadModule php_module "c:/php/php7apache2_4.dll"

AddHandler application/x-httpd-php .php

PHPIniDir "C:/php"

Ensure the path to your PHP installation matches the

directory where you extracted PHP.

Install phpMyAdmin:
Download phpMyAdmin from the phpMyAdmin website. Extract it to the htdocs directory (e.g., C:\Apache24\htdocs\phpmyadmin).

Rename the configuration file:
Copy config.sample.inc.php to config.inc.php

Open the config.inc.php file and set the configuration for your database connection:

$cfg['Servers'][$i]['host'] = 'localhost';

$cfg['Servers'][$i]['user'] = 'root';

$cfg['Servers'][$i]['password'] = '';

Access phpMyAdmin by navigating to http://localhost/phpmyadmin.

Installing Java (JDK) and Configuring MariaDB/MySQL with Apache/Nginx on Windows

If you're developing Java applications that need to interact with a database like MariaDB/MySQL, you'll also need to install Java and configure the necessary components.

Installation for Java, MariaDB/MySQL, and Apache/Nginx on Windows

Install Java Development Kit (JDK):

Go to the Oracle JDK download page. Download the appropriate JDK version for Windows. Run the installer and follow the instructions to install the JDK.

Set up Java environment variables:

Open **System Properties** > **Advanced** > **Environment Variables**

Add a new system variable:

Variable Name: JAVA_HOME

Variable Value: Path to your JDK installation directory (e.g., C:\Program Files\Java\jdk-11).

Add the bin directory of your JDK to the Path variable (e.g., C:\Program Files\Java\jdk-11\bin).

Install MariaDB/MySQL:

If you haven't installed MariaDB yet, download the installer from the MariaDB website. Run the installer and follow the instructions. Secure the installation by setting a root password when prompted.

Install Apache or Nginx:

Apache: Follow the same steps as outlined in the previous section for installing Apache.

Nginx: If you prefer to use Nginx, you can download the Windows version of Nginx from the official website.

Extract the files to a directory (e.g., C:\nginx).

Open the command prompt, navigate to the Nginx directory, and run:

start nginx

Set Up JDBC for Java to Connect to MariaDB (MySQL):

Download the MariaDB JDBC driver. Place the downloaded .jar file in your project directory or Java classpath. Modify your Java code to load the JDBC driver and establish a connection to your MariaDB database.

Example Java code for connecting to MariaDB (MySQL):

```java
import java.sql.*;

public class Main {
    public static void main(String[] args) {
        String url = "jdbc:mariadb://localhost:3306/YourDatabaseName";
        String user = "YourUserName";
        String password = "YourPassword";

        try {
            // Load JDBC driver
            Class.forName("org.mariadb.jdbc.Driver");

            // Establish a connection
            Connection con = DriverManager.getConnection(url, user, password);
```

```java
        // Execute queries
        Statement stmt = con.createStatement();
        ResultSet rs = stmt.executeQuery("SELECT * FROM
YourTable");

        while (rs.next()) {
            System.out.println(rs.getString(1));
            // Example: print first column of results

        }

        // Close resources
        rs.close();
        stmt.close();
        con.close();
    } catch (SQLException | ClassNotFoundException e) {
        e.printStackTrace();
    }
  }
}
```

Chapter 3: Connecting to MariaDB (MySQL) with PDO

Connecting to a MariaDB (MySQL) database with PDO (PHP Data Objects) is crucial because it allows your PHP application to securely and efficiently interact with the database. For example, if your database stores a list of users with names and addresses, your PHP programs can use PDO to easily retrieve, add, or update that information.

PDO simplifies these tasks by providing a standardized way to work with different types of databases. It also supports powerful features like prepared statements, which enhance security by protecting your application against SQL injection attacks. Additionally, PDO offers flexibility, allowing you to switch to other databases (such as PostgreSQL or SQLite) with minimal changes to your code.

If you haven't yet created a database and user for your application, please revisit **Chapter 1: Setting Up Your Development Environment**. There, you'll find step-by-step instructions on how to create your first database, set up a user, and grant that user access to the database.

Connecting to MariaDB (MySQL) with PDO in PHP Scripts

Connecting to a MariaDB (MySQL) database with PDO (PHP Data Objects) is a secure and efficient way to handle database interactions in PHP.

To ensure that your PHP and Java examples work correctly, you will need a MySQL database with a table named **Test_Table** and two columns named **id** and **Test_Column**. Below are step-by-step instructions for creating this table via both the command-line interface (CLI) and on Windows.

Creating a MySQL Table & Column using CLI

Open Terminal: Open the terminal or command line interface on your system.

Login to MySQL: You need to log in to your MySQL server using the MySQL root user or another user with sufficient privileges.

mysql -u root -p

You will be prompted to enter the MySQL root password.

Select a Database: If you haven't already created the database named **YourDatabaseName**, you need to create it first. If you already have created this database, skip this step and select your existing database.

CREATE DATABASE YourDatabaseName;

USE YourDatabaseName;

Create a table named **Test_Table** with two columns named, **id** and **Test_Column**.

The **id** column will automatically increment with each new record, serving as a unique identifier for each row. The **Test_Column** will be of type VARCHAR(255), allowing it to store text data with a maximum length of 255 characters.

```
CREATE TABLE Test_Table (
        id INT AUTO_INCREMENT PRIMARY KEY,
        Test_Column VARCHAR(255)
);
```

Verify the Table Creation: You can check if the table was created by listing all tables:

SHOW TABLES;

Exit MySQL: After the table is created, you can exit MySQL:

EXIT;

Creating a MySQL Table using MySQL Workbench (Windows)

Open MySQL Workbench: Launch MySQL Workbench on your Windows machine.

Connect to the MySQL Server:

Open MySQL Workbench and connect to your MySQL server using your MySQL username and password.

Create a Database:

In the "**Navigator**" panel, click on the **+** icon to create a new schema (database). Provide the name for your database (e.g., **YourDatabaseName**), and click Apply to create the database.

Create the Table:

After the database is created, click on it in the Navigator to select it.

Open a new SQL tab by clicking on the SQL button.

Enter the following SQL query to create the table named **Test_Table** with two columns named **id** and **Test_Column**:

```
CREATE TABLE Test_Table (
        id INT AUTO_INCREMENT PRIMARY KEY,
        Test_Column VARCHAR(255)
);
```

Click Execute (the lightning bolt icon) to run the query and create the table.

Verify the Table Creation:

You can view the created table in the Schemas section on the left, under your database. Right-click on Tables and select Refresh to see **Test_Table** appear in the list.

Creating a MySQL Table Using PHPMyAdmin (Windows or Linux)

Open PHPMyAdmin:

Open your web browser and go to phpMyAdmin. This is typically available at http://localhost/phpmyadmin if you're running a local server like XAMPP or WAMP.

If you are using a live server, navigate to the phpMyAdmin URL provided by your hosting provider.

Select/Create a Database:

Once you are logged into phpMyAdmin, click on the **"Databases"** tab at the top of the screen.

If you already have a database (e.g., **YourDatabaseName**), you can simply click on it in the list on the left.

If you need to create a new database:

In the **"Create database"** field, type the desired name for your database (e.g., **YourDatabaseName**).

Select the collation type (use utf8_general_ci for general purposes).

Click **Create**.

Create the Table:

After selecting or creating your database, you will be taken to the **Structure tab** where you can manage the tables in your database.

In the **"Create table"** section, enter the name of your table (e.g., **Test_Table**).

Specify the number of columns you want (in this case, 2 columns:

id and **Test_Column**).

Click **Go**.

Define the Columns:

You will be taken to a screen where you can define the columns for your table.

For Column 1 (id):

Name: id

Type: INT

Length/Values: Leave it at **11** (default for integers).

Attributes: Check **AUTO_INCREMENT** (this automatically increments the value for each new record).

Index: Select **PRIMARY** (this makes the **id** column the **primary key**).

For Column 2 (Test_Column):

Name: Test_Column

Type: VARCHAR

Length/Values: Set this to **255** (this specifies the maximum number of characters the column can store).

Your table structure will look like this:

Column Name	Type	Length/Values	Attributes	Index
id	INT	11	AUTO_INCREMENT	PRIMARY
Test_Column	VARCHAR	255		

Save the Table:

Scroll down and click Save to create the table. phpMyAdmin will create the table and display a confirmation message.

Verify the Table:

After saving, phpMyAdmin will automatically show the table structure, and you can now start inserting data into the table or manage it further using the other tabs (Browse, SQL, etc.).

Explanation

The **id** column is of type INT with the AUTO_INCREMENT and PRIMARY key attributes, which will automatically assign unique values to the column and serve as the primary identifier for each row.

The **Test_Column** is of type VARCHAR with a length of 255 characters, allowing it to store text.

Establish a connection to MySQL Using PHP

If you haven't yet created a database named
YourDatabaseName with a table **Test_Table** and two
columns named **id** and **Test_Column**, please refer to Chapter
3 for instructions on creating a MySQL table and column. You
can choose from the following sections:

Chapter 3: Creating a MySQL Table & Column using CLI

Chapter 3: Creating a MySQL Table using MySQL Workbench
(Windows)

Chapter 3: Creating a MySQL Table Using PHPMyAdmin
(Windows or Linux)

Once you've completed these steps, you can proceed with
connecting to the database.

Create the following text file using a simple text editor like
Notepad or Bluefish on Windows or nano on Linux:

```php
<?php

// The hostname (usually localhost for local development)
$host = 'localhost';
$dbname = 'YourDatabaseName';  // The name of your database
$username = 'YourUserName';  // Your database username
$password = 'YourPassword';  // Your database password


try {
        // Create a new PDO instance
        $pdo = new PDO("mysql:host=$host;dbname=$dbname",
        $username, $password);
```

```php
        // Set PDO to throw exceptions in case of errors
        $pdo->setAttribute(PDO::ATTR_ERRMODE,
PDO::ERRMODE_EXCEPTION);

        echo "Connected successfully!";

} catch (PDOException $e) {
        // Handle connection errors
        echo "Connection failed: " . $e->getMessage();
}

?>
```

Save the file as: db-connect.php

Explanation

PDO Object: The new PDO() line is where you establish the connection. It takes three parameters:

mysql:host=$host: This specifies the host (usually localhost).

dbname=$dbname: This is the name of the database you're connecting to.

$username and $password: These are the credentials for accessing the database.

Error Handling: The setAttribute(PDO::ATTR_ERRMODE, PDO::ERRMODE_EXCEPTION); line ensures that PDO will throw exceptions if something goes wrong. This is important for debugging and securing your application.

Try/Catch Block: The try block attempts to connect to the database, and the catch block catches any exceptions, printing an error message if the connection fails.

Executing db-connect.php

Open a web browser and type the following URL:

http://localhost/db-connect.php

If you uploaded your db-connect.php to your website or to a remote server:

http://yourdomain.com/db-connect.php

If you placed the file in a folder, make sure to include the folder name in the URL (e.g., http://localhost/folder/db-connect.php).

If the connection is successful, the browser should display:

Connected successfully!

If there's an issue with the connection (incorrect database credentials, MySQL not running, etc.), an error message will be displayed, such as:

Connection failed: [error message].

Establish a connection to MySQL Using Java

In Java, connecting to a MariaDB (MySQL) database using PDO-like functionality is achieved through JDBC (Java Database Connectivity), which serves as the standard interface for database access in Java. While Java does not have a direct equivalent of PHP's PDO, it uses the JDBC API to connect to databases in a similarly flexible and secure way. JDBC allows developers to establish a connection to the database, execute SQL queries, and retrieve results.

The process involves loading the MariaDB (MySQL) driver, establishing a connection using DriverManager, and handling data with Statement or PreparedStatement objects. Just like PDO in PHP, JDBC in Java supports prepared statements, which help prevent SQL injection attacks, making it a secure and efficient way to interact with databases. JDBC also offers flexibility, allowing Java applications to connect to various database types by simply changing the connection URL and driver.

If you haven't yet created a database named **YourDatabaseName** with a table **Test_Table** and two columns named **id** and **Test_Column**, please refer to Chapter 3 for instructions on creating a MySQL table and column. You can choose from the following sections:

Chapter 3: Creating a MySQL Table & Column using CLI

Chapter 3: Creating a MySQL Table using MySQL Workbench (Windows)

Chapter 3: Creating a MySQL Table Using PHPMyAdmin (Windows or Linux)

Once you've completed these steps, you can proceed with connecting to the database with the example below.

Connect to a MySQL Database Using JDBC in Java

You can follow these steps to connect to a MySQL database in Java using JDBC (Java Database Connectivity). You can create a Java file using any text editor like Notepad on Windows, or nano on Linux. Below is a full example of connecting to MySQL:

```
import java.sql.*;

public class DBConnect {
    public static void main(String[] args) {

        // Database credentials (replace these with your actual details)
        String url = "jdbc:mysql://localhost:3306/YourDatabaseName";
        // Database URL (change above to  YourDatabaseName)

        String user = "YourUserName";  // MySQL username
        String password = "YourPassword";  // MySQL password

        // Connection and statement objects
        Connection con = null;
        Statement stmt = null;
        ResultSet rs = null;

        try {
            // Step 1: Register the MySQL JDBC driver - required for
            //  MySQL 5.x, optional for MySQL 8+)
            // Class.forName("com.mysql.cj.jdbc.Driver");
```

```java
    // Uncomment above for MySQL 5.x or older if needed

    // Step 2: Establish the connection to the database
    con = DriverManager.getConnection(url, user, password);
    System.out.println("Connected successfully!");

    // Step 3: Create a Statement object to execute SQL queries
    stmt = con.createStatement();

    // Step 4: Execute a query (Modify this to use your actual table
    // and columns)
    String query = "SELECT * FROM Test_Table";
    // Replace Test_Table with your actual table name above

    rs = stmt.executeQuery(query);

    // Step 5: Process the result set
    while (rs.next()) {
        // Assuming your table has a column 'Test_Column'
        System.out.println("Data: " + rs.getString("Test_Column"));
        // Replace 'Test_Column' with your column name above
    }

} catch (SQLException e) {
    // Handle SQL errors
    e.printStackTrace();
} catch (ClassNotFoundException e) {
    // Handle errors for missing JDBC driver
    e.printStackTrace();
} finally {
    // Step 6: Close resources in the finally block to avoid resource
    // leaks
    try {
        if (rs != null) rs.close();
        if (stmt != null) stmt.close();
        if (con != null) con.close();
    } catch (SQLException se) {
        se.printStackTrace();
    }
}
}
}
```

Save the file as: DBConnect.java

Explanation

JDBC Driver Registration:

The line Class.forName("com.mysql.cj.jdbc.Driver"); is used to load the MySQL JDBC driver. This step is not required for MySQL 8.0 and newer versions, as the driver is automatically registered. However, it is essential for older versions like MySQL 5.x.

Establish Connection:

The DriverManager.getConnection(url, user, password) method establishes the connection to the MySQL database using the provided database URL, username, and password.

Create a Statement:

After establishing the connection, a Statement object is created to send SQL queries to the database.

Executing Queries:

The query "SELECT * FROM Test_Table" is executed to retrieve all records from the specified table (Test_Table). You can replace Test_Table with your actual table name.

Process Result Set:

The ResultSet object (rs) stores the query results. The rs.next() method is used to iterate through the rows, and rs.getString("Test_Column") retrieves the data from the column Test_Column (replace it with your actual column name).

Exception Handling:

SQL and ClassNotFound exceptions are caught and printed to the console. You should always include exception handling when working with database connections to capture any errors.

Resource Management:

The resources (ResultSet, Statement, Connection) are closed in the finally block to prevent resource leaks. This ensures the program cleans up after itself.

Requirements:

MySQL JDBC Driver:

You need to include the MySQL JDBC driver in your project. For MySQL 8.0 and later, you need the mysql-connector-java JAR file.

If you're using **Maven** to manage your project dependencies, you can add the following dependency to your **pom.xml**:

```
<dependency>
    <groupId>mysql</groupId>
    <artifactId>mysql-connector-java</artifactId>
    <version>8.0.29</version> <!-- Use the latest version -->
</dependency>
```

Compiling and Running the Program

Open Command Line/Terminal:

On **Windows**, open the Command Prompt or PowerShell.

On **Linux**, open your terminal.

Navigate to the Directory:

Use the cd command to navigate to the folder where your DBConnect.java file is located.

Compile the Java Program

Use the javac command to compile your Java program:

javac DBConnect.java

This will generate a DBConnect.class file in the same directory.

Run the Compiled Program:

After compiling successfully, run the program using the java command:

java DBConnect

This will execute the main method and attempt to connect

to your MySQL database.

Expected Output:

If the connection is successful, you should see output like:

Connected successfully!

Data: [column_value]

If there's an issue (like incorrect credentials or the database not running), you might see an error message like:

Connection failed: [error message]

Chapter 4: Performing CRUD Operations

CRUD stands for **Create, Read, Update, and Delete**, which are the basic operations used to manage data in a database. These operations are essential for interacting with any database-driven application. Whether you're working with MySQL through PHP or Java, performing CRUD operations is a core part of developing dynamic websites or applications.

Create: This operation allows you to add new records to your database. In PHP, you can use the INSERT INTO SQL statement to insert data, while in Java, you would use PreparedStatement to prevent SQL injection and safely insert values into your table.

Read: The Read operation retrieves data from the database using the SELECT statement. In PHP, this is typically done with PDO's query() method, while in Java, the ResultSet object is used to process the data returned from a SELECT query.

Update: This operation modifies existing records in the database. Using the UPDATE statement, you can change the values of specific columns based on a condition. Both PHP and Java support parameterized queries for updates, which helps ensure the security of your application by preventing SQL injection attacks.

Delete: The Delete operation allows you to remove records from your database. By using the DELETE statement, you can specify a condition to delete specific rows. It's important to be careful with this operation to avoid accidentally deleting important data.

These CRUD operations are fundamental when interacting with databases. Understanding how to properly execute them in PHP and Java ensures that your application can effectively create, access, update, and remove data as needed.

Create (INSERT Data)

The Create operation in CRUD refers to inserting new records into a database. It's essential to securely insert data to avoid common vulnerabilities like SQL injection. Both PHP and Java provide ways to securely insert data using prepared statements. Here's how you can securely insert data in both languages:

Inserting Data Using Prepared Statements in PHP

In PHP, PDO (PHP Data Objects) can be used to securely interact with a MySQL database. Prepared statements ensure user input is handled safely by separating the SQL logic from the data, thus preventing SQL injection attacks where malicious SQL code might be inserted into user inputs.

Create db-connect.php

To establish a connection to your MySQL database, first

create a **db-connect.php** text file. This file will use PDO to securely handle the interaction with the database:

```php
<?php

// Database connection details
$host = 'localhost';
$dbname = 'YourDatabaseName';  // Replace with your database name
$username = 'YourUserName';    // Replace with your database username
$password = 'YourPassword';    // Replace with your database password

try {
    // Create a new PDO instance
    $pdo = new PDO("mysql:host=$host;dbname=$dbname", $username, $password);

    // Set PDO to throw exceptions in case of errors
    $pdo->setAttribute(PDO::ATTR_ERRMODE, PDO::ERRMODE_EXCEPTION);

    echo "Connected successfully!";
} catch (PDOException $e) {
    // Handle connection errors
    echo "Connection failed: " . $e->getMessage();
}

?>
```

Save the file as db-connect.php.

Create insert-data.php

In this example, we demonstrate how to securely insert data into your database using prepared statements in PHP.

```php
<?php

// Include the database connection script
include("db-connect.php");

try {
    // Prepare the SQL statement with a placeholder for the value
    $stmt = $pdo->prepare("INSERT INTO Test_Table (Test_Column) VALUES (:test_value)");

    // Bind the actual data to the placeholder
    $stmt->bindParam(':test_value', $test_value, PDO::PARAM_STR);

    // Example value to insert (you would use user input in a real
    // scenario)
    $test_value = "Sample Data";

    // Execute the prepared statement
    $stmt->execute();

    echo "Data inserted successfully!";
} catch (PDOException $e) {
    echo "Error: " . $e->getMessage();
}

?>
```

Save the file as insert-data.php.

Breakdown of the Code

Database Connection:

The script starts by including the db-connect.php file, which contains the database connection details and establishes a PDO connection to the MySQL database.

Prepare the SQL Statement:

The SQL INSERT statement is prepared with a placeholder :test_value. This placeholder is where the actual data will be inserted.

Bind Parameters:

The $stmt->bindParam() function binds the value of $test_value to the placeholder :test_value. This step ensures the data is safely passed into the SQL statement, preventing SQL injection attacks.

Execute the Statement:

The prepared statement is executed with $stmt->execute(), which performs the actual insertion of data into the database.

Result:

If the statement executes successfully, the message "Data inserted successfully!" is displayed. If any errors occur during the process, they are caught and displayed as an error message.

How to Run the PHP script:

Open your browser and visit:

http://localhost/ db-connect.php

Inserting Data Using Prepared Statements in Java

Inserting data using prepared statements in Java is a secure and efficient way to interact with a database. By using a PreparedStatement, you can prevent SQL injection attacks and improve performance by allowing the database to pre-compile the SQL query. In this approach, the SQL statement is prepared with placeholders for the data values, which are later bound to the statement before execution. This separation of query structure from data ensures that user input is treated as data rather than executable code, enhancing security. Additionally, prepared statements are reusable, meaning the same query can be executed multiple times with different data, making it more efficient than using simple Statement objects. The process typically involves creating a database connection, preparing the query, binding parameters, executing the statement, and handling exceptions and resource cleanup.

This java code demonstrates how to separate the database connection logic into a DBConnect.java file. The connection is then used in the main PdoInsert.java class to insert data securely using prepared statements.

Create DBConnect.java

First, create the DBConnect.java file, which handles the connection to the MySQL database.

```java
import java.sql.Connection;
import java.sql.DriverManager;
import java.sql.SQLException;

public class DBConnect {

    // Method to establish a connection to the database
    public static Connection getConnection() {
        String url = "jdbc:mysql://localhost:3306/YourDatabaseName";
        // Replace above with your database URL

        String user = "YourUserName";
        // Replace above with your database username

        String password = "YourPassword";
        // Replace above with your database password

        Connection con = null;

        try {
            // Establish the connection to the database
            con = DriverManager.getConnection(url, user, password);
        } catch (SQLException e) {
            System.out.println("Connection failed: " + e.getMessage());
        }
        return con;
    }
}
```

Save the file as DBConnect.java.

Create PdoInsert.java

Next, create the PdoInsert.java file, which imports the DBConnect class and inserts data into the database using a prepared statement.

```java
import java.sql.*;

public class PdoInsert {
    public static void main(String[] args) {

        // Connection object and PreparedStatement
        Connection con = null;
        PreparedStatement stmt = null;

        try {
            // Use the DBConnect class to establish the connection
            con = DBConnect.getConnection();

            if (con != null) {
                // Prepare the SQL statement with a placeholder
                String sql = "INSERT INTO Test_Table (Test_Column) VALUES (?)";

                stmt = con.prepareStatement(sql);

                // Set the value for the placeholder
                stmt.setString(1, "Sample Data");

                // Execute the statement
                stmt.executeUpdate();

                System.out.println("Data inserted successfully!");
            } else {
                System.out.println("Failed to establish connection.");
            }

        } catch (SQLException e) {
            System.out.println("Error during SQL operation: " +
e.getMessage());

        } finally {
            // Close resources
            try {
                if (stmt != null) stmt.close();
                if (con != null) con.close();
            } catch (SQLException se) {
                System.out.println("Error closing resources: " +
se.getMessage());
            }
```

```
        }
    }
}
```

Save the file as PdoInsert.java.

Explanation

DBConnect.java:

Functionality: This class handles the database connection logic. It has a static method getConnection() that returns a Connection object.

Customization: The connection parameters (url, user, password) are hardcoded. For added flexibility, you could modify it to read from a configuration file or environment variables.

PdoInsert.java:

Functionality: This class connects to the database using DBConnect.getConnection(), prepares an SQL INSERT statement with a placeholder, binds a value to the placeholder, and executes the statement.

Error Handling: It includes error handling to catch and display any SQL exceptions.

Resource Management: Ensures that the resources (PreparedStatement and Connection) are properly closed in the finally block.

How to Compile and Run

Compile the classes:

javac DBConnect.java PdoInsert.java

Run the main class:

java PdoInsert

This structure makes it easier to manage the database connection and reuse it across different parts of your application. Instead of duplicating connection code in multiple classes, you can simply call DBConnect.getConnection() whenever a database connection is needed.

Read (SELECT Data)

Reading (SELECT Data) in a database involves querying the database to retrieve specific information. In PHP, this can be done securely using prepared statements, which prevent SQL injection by separating the SQL query from user input. The process starts by preparing a SELECT query with placeholders for the parameters. These placeholders are then bound to actual values, ensuring safe data handling.

Once the statement is executed, the results can be fetched using methods like fetchAll(), which retrieves the data in an associative array format. This approach helps maintain both

security and efficiency in database operations, ensuring that the data retrieval is done without exposing the application to potential vulnerabilities.

Read (SELECT Data) Using Prepared Statements in PHP

In PHP, PDO (PHP Data Objects) can be used to securely interact with a MySQL database. Prepared statements ensure user input is handled safely by separating the SQL logic from the data, thus preventing SQL injection attacks where malicious SQL code might be inserted into user inputs. This is particularly useful when retrieving data from a database, where user input might affect the query results. Before proceeding, ensure you have the db-connect.php file created, which will handle the database connection.

Create db-connect.php

To establish a connection to your MySQL database, create a **db-connect.php** text file. This file will use PDO to securely handle the interaction with the database:

```php
<?php

// Database connection details
$host = 'localhost';
$dbname = 'YourDatabaseName';  // Replace with your database name
$username = 'YourUserName';    // Replace with your database username
$password = 'YourPassword';    // Replace with your database password

try {
    // Create a new PDO instance
    $pdo = new PDO("mysql:host=$host;dbname=$dbname", $username, $password);

    // Set PDO to throw exceptions in case of errors
    $pdo->setAttribute(PDO::ATTR_ERRMODE, PDO::ERRMODE_EXCEPTION);

    echo "Connected successfully!";
} catch (PDOException $e) {
    // Handle connection errors
    echo "Connection failed: " . $e->getMessage();
}

?>
```

Save the file as db-connect.php.

Create select-data.php

In this example, we demonstrate how to securely read data from your database using prepared statements in PHP.

```php
<?php

// Include the database connection script
include("db-connect.php");

try {
    // Prepare the SQL SELECT statement with a placeholder for the
value
    $stmt = $pdo->prepare("SELECT * FROM Test_Table WHERE
Test_Column = :test_value");

    // Bind the actual data to the placeholder
    $stmt->bindParam(':test_value', $test_value, PDO::PARAM_STR);

    // Example value to search (you would use user input in a real
    // scenario)
    $test_value = "Sample Data";

    // Execute the prepared statement
    $stmt->execute();

    // Fetch the results
    $results = $stmt->fetchAll(PDO::FETCH_ASSOC);

    // Check if there are results
    if ($results) {
        foreach ($results as $row) {
            // Output the result (you can customize this as needed)
            echo "Test Column: " . $row['Test_Column'] . "<br>";
        }
    } else {
        echo "No data found!";
    }

} catch (PDOException $e) {
    echo "Error: " . $e->getMessage();
}

?>
```

Save the file as select-data.php.

Breakdown of the Code

Database Connection:

The script starts by including the db-connect.php file, which contains the database connection details and establishes a PDO connection to the MySQL database.

Prepare the SQL Statement:

The SQL SELECT statement is prepared with a placeholder :test_value. This placeholder is where the actual data will be used in the query, ensuring safe handling of user input.

Bind Parameters:

The $stmt->bindParam() function binds the value of $test_value to the placeholder :test_value. This step ensures that the data is safely passed into the SQL query, preventing SQL injection attacks.

Execute the Statement:

The prepared statement is executed with $stmt->execute(), which performs the actual query to fetch data from the database.

Fetch and Display Results:

The query results are fetched using **$stmt->fetchAll(PDO::FETCH_ASSOC)**, which retrieves all rows as an associative array. The data is then displayed to the user, or a message indicating no results is shown.

How to Run the PHP Script

Open your browser and visit:

http://localhost/select-data.php

This will execute the PHP script, connect to the MySQL database, and display the data retrieved from the Test_Table where the value of Test_Column matches the test_value.

Read (SELECT Data) Using Prepared Statements in Java

Reading data from a database securely using prepared statements in Java helps prevent SQL injection attacks and enhances performance. A PreparedStatement is used to execute SQL queries with placeholders for parameters. By using this approach, user input is handled safely, ensuring that input values are treated as data, not executable code. Prepared statements are reusable, allowing multiple executions of the same query with different data, improving efficiency.

In this example, we separate the database connection logic into a DBConnect.java file. The connection is then used in the main PdoSelect.java class to read data from the database securely using prepared statements.

Create DBConnect.java

First, create the **DBConnect.java** text file, which handles the connection to the MySQL database:

```java
import java.sql.Connection;
import java.sql.DriverManager;
import java.sql.SQLException;

public class DBConnect {

    // Method to establish a connection to the database
    public static Connection getConnection() {
        String url = "jdbc:mysql://localhost:3306/YourDatabaseName";
        // Replace above with your database URL

        String user = "YourUserName";
        // Replace above with your database username

        String password = "YourPassword";
        // Replace above with your database password

        Connection con = null;

        try {
            // Establish the connection to the database
            con = DriverManager.getConnection(url, user, password);
        } catch (SQLException e) {
            System.out.println("Connection failed: " + e.getMessage());
        }
        return con;
    }
}
```

Save the file as DBConnect.java.

Create PdoSelect.java

Next, create the PdoSelect.java file, which imports the DBConnect class and retrieves data from the database using a prepared statement:

```java
import java.sql.*;

public class PdoSelect {
    public static void main(String[] args) {

        // Connection object and PreparedStatement
        Connection con = null;
        PreparedStatement stmt = null;
        ResultSet rs = null;

        try {
            // Use the DBConnect class to establish the connection
            con = DBConnect.getConnection();

            if (con != null) {

                // Prepare the SQL SELECT statement with a placeholder
                String sql = "SELECT Test_Column FROM Test_Table WHERE id = ?";

                stmt = con.prepareStatement(sql);

                // Set the value for the placeholder
                stmt.setInt(1, 1);  // Example: Fetching the row with id = 1

                // Execute the query
                rs = stmt.executeQuery();

                // Process the result set
                if (rs.next()) {
                    String data = rs.getString("Test_Column");
                    System.out.println("Data retrieved: " + data);
```

```
        } else {
            System.out.println("No data found for the given id.");
        }
    } else {
        System.out.println("Failed to establish connection.");
    }

} catch (SQLException e) {
    System.out.println("Error during SQL operation: " +
e.getMessage());

} finally {
    // Close resources
    try {
        if (rs != null) rs.close();
        if (stmt != null) stmt.close();
        if (con != null) con.close();
    } catch (SQLException se) {
        System.out.println("Error closing resources: " +
se.getMessage());

        }
    }
  }
}
```

Save the file as PdoSelect.java.

Explanation

DBConnect.java:

Functionality: This class handles the database connection logic. It has a static method getConnection() that returns a Connection object for connecting to the database.

Customization: The connection parameters (URL, username, password) are hardcoded, but you can modify this to read from a configuration file or environment variables for flexibility.

PdoSelect.java:

Functionality: This class connects to the database using DBConnect.getConnection(), prepares an SQL SELECT statement with a placeholder, binds a value to the placeholder, and retrieves the result using a ResultSet.

Error Handling: It includes error handling for SQL exceptions.

Resource Management: Ensures that resources such as the ResultSet, PreparedStatement, and Connection are properly closed in the finally block.

How to Compile and Run

Compile the classes:

javac DBConnect.java PdoSelect.java

Run the main class:

java PdoSelect

This will execute the PdoSelect class, connect to the database, and retrieve data from the Test_Table where the id matches the specified value (1 in this case).

Update (UPDATE Data)

The UPDATE operation in MySQL using PDO (PHP Data Objects) allows you to modify existing records in a table securely and efficiently. Using prepared statements with PDO is crucial for preventing SQL injection attacks by separating the SQL query from user inputs. To perform an update, you first establish a connection to the MySQL database, prepare an SQL UPDATE query with placeholders for the values you want to modify, bind the actual data to these placeholders, and then execute the query. After execution, you can check how many rows were affected to verify if the operation was successful. This method ensures that user inputs are safely handled and that the connection and prepared statements are properly managed to prevent

resource leaks.

Update (UPDATE Data) Using Prepared Statements in PHP

In PHP, PDO (PHP Data Objects) can be used to securely interact with a MySQL database. Prepared statements ensure user input is handled safely by separating the SQL logic from the data, thus preventing SQL injection attacks where malicious SQL code might be inserted into user inputs. This is especially important when updating data in a database, where user input could potentially affect the query. Before proceeding, ensure you have the db-connect.php file created, which will handle the database connection.

Create db-connect.php

To establish a connection to your MySQL database, create a **db-connect.php** file. This file will use PDO to securely handle the interaction with the database:

```php
<?php

// Database connection details
$host = 'localhost';
$dbname = 'YourDatabaseName';  // Replace with your database name
$username = 'YourUserName';    // Replace with your database username
$password = 'YourPassword';    // Replace with your database password

try {
    // Create a new PDO instance
    $pdo = new PDO("mysql:host=$host;dbname=$dbname", $username, $password);

    // Set PDO to throw exceptions in case of errors
    $pdo->setAttribute(PDO::ATTR_ERRMODE, PDO::ERRMODE_EXCEPTION);

    echo "Connected successfully!";
} catch (PDOException $e) {
    // Handle connection errors
    echo "Connection failed: " . $e->getMessage();
}
```

```
?>
```

Save the file as db-connect.php.

Create update-data.php

In this example, we create a text file named **update-data.php** which demonstrates how to securely update data in your database using prepared statements in PHP.

```php
<?php

// Include the database connection script
include("db-connect.php");

try {
    // Prepare the SQL UPDATE statement with placeholders for the
values
    $stmt = $pdo->prepare("UPDATE Test_Table SET Test_Column =
:test_value WHERE id = :record_id");

    // Bind the actual data to the placeholders
    $stmt->bindParam(':test_value', $test_value, PDO::PARAM_STR);
    $stmt->bindParam(':record_id', $record_id, PDO::PARAM_INT);

    // Example values to update (you would use user input in a real
    // scenario)
    $test_value = "Updated Data";
    $record_id = 1;

    // Execute the prepared statement
    $stmt->execute();

    echo "Data updated successfully!";
} catch (PDOException $e) {
    echo "Error: " . $e->getMessage();
}

?>
```

Save the file as update-data.php.

Breakdown of the Code

Database Connection:

The script starts by including the db-connect.php file, which

contains the database connection details and establishes a PDO connection to the MySQL database.

Prepare the SQL Statement:

The SQL UPDATE statement is prepared with placeholders :test_value and :record_id. These placeholders are where the actual data will be inserted into the query, ensuring safe handling of user input.

Bind Parameters:

The $stmt->bindParam() function binds the values of $test_value and $record_id to the placeholders :test_value and :record_id. This step ensures the data is safely passed into the SQL statement, preventing SQL injection attacks.

Execute the Statement:

The prepared statement is executed with $stmt->execute(), which performs the actual update operation in the database.

Result:

If the statement executes successfully, the message "Data updated successfully!" is displayed. If any errors occur during the process, they are caught and displayed as an error message.

How to Run the Script:

Open your browser and visit:

http://localhost/update-data.php

This will execute the PHP script, connect to the MySQL database, and update the data in the Test_Table where the id matches the record_id, setting the value of Test_Column to test_value.

Update (UPDATE Data) Using Prepared Statements in Java

Updating data in a database securely and efficiently using prepared statements in Java is crucial for preventing SQL injection attacks and improving performance. By using a PreparedStatement, you can safely bind user input to SQL queries, ensuring that input is treated as data rather than executable code. Prepared statements also improve performance by allowing the database to pre-compile the SQL query, making it reusable for multiple executions.

In this example, we separate the database connection logic into a DBConnect.java file, and the update operation is handled in the main PdoUpdate.java class.

Create DBConnect.java

First, create the DBConnect.java file, which manages the connection to the MySQL database:

```java
import java.sql.Connection;
import java.sql.DriverManager;
import java.sql.SQLException;

public class DBConnect {

    // Method to establish a connection to the database
    public static Connection getConnection() {
        String url = "jdbc:mysql://localhost:3306/YourDatabaseName";
        // Replace above with your database URL

        String user = "YourUserName";
        // Replace above with your database username

        String password = "YourPassword";
        // Replace above with your database password

        Connection con = null;

        try {
            // Establish the connection to the database
            con = DriverManager.getConnection(url, user, password);
        } catch (SQLException e) {
            System.out.println("Connection failed: " + e.getMessage());
        }
        return con;
    }
}
```

Save the file as DBConnect.java.

Create PdoUpdate.java

Next, create the PdoUpdate.java file, which uses the DBConnect class and performs the data update operation using a prepared statement:

```java
import java.sql.*;

public class PdoUpdate {
    public static void main(String[] args) {

        // Connection object and PreparedStatement
        Connection con = null;
        PreparedStatement stmt = null;

        try {
            // Use the DBConnect class to establish the connection
            con = DBConnect.getConnection();

            if (con != null) {
                // Prepare the SQL UPDATE statement with placeholders
                String sql = "UPDATE Test_Table SET Test_Column = ? WHERE id = ?";

                stmt = con.prepareStatement(sql);

                // Set the values for the placeholders
                stmt.setString(1, "Updated Data");
                // New value above for the column

                stmt.setInt(2, 1);  // ID of the record to update

                // Execute the update statement
                int rowsAffected = stmt.executeUpdate();

                if (rowsAffected > 0) {
                    System.out.println("Data updated successfully!");
                } else {
```

```
                System.out.println("No record found with the specified
id.");

            }
        } else {
            System.out.println("Failed to establish connection.");
        }

    } catch (SQLException e) {
        System.out.println("Error during SQL operation: " +
e.getMessage());

    } finally {
        // Close resources
        try {
            if (stmt != null) stmt.close();
            if (con != null) con.close();
        } catch (SQLException se) {
            System.out.println("Error closing resources: " +
se.getMessage());
        }
    }
  }
}
```

Save the file as PdoUpdate.java.

Explanation

DBConnect.java:

Functionality: This class handles the database connection logic. It provides a static method getConnection() that returns a Connection object for connecting to the MySQL database.

Customization: The connection parameters (URL, username, password) are hardcoded for simplicity, but these can be customized to read from a configuration file or environment variables.

PdoUpdate.java:

Functionality: This class connects to the database using DBConnect.getConnection(), prepares an SQL UPDATE statement with placeholders, binds values to the placeholders, and then executes the statement.

Error Handling: The code includes error handling to catch and display SQL exceptions.

Resource Management: The finally block ensures that resources (like PreparedStatement and Connection) are properly closed after the operation.

How to Compile and Run

Compile the classes:

javac DBConnect.java PdoUpdate.java

Run the main class:

java PdoUpdate

This will execute the PdoUpdate class, which will connect to the database and update the Test_Table where the id matches 1, changing the value in the Test_Column to

"Updated Data".

Delete (DELETE Data)

Deleting data using prepared statements in SQL is a secure and efficient method for removing records from a database. By using prepared statements, the SQL query is pre-compiled with placeholders for the values to be deleted, preventing SQL injection attacks and ensuring that user input is treated safely as data, not executable code. The DELETE statement typically specifies conditions (such as an ID) to identify which records to remove. Prepared statements enhance performance by allowing the database to optimize and reuse

the query execution plan. This approach not only improves security but also streamlines the database interaction process, making it more efficient and less error-prone.

Delete (DELETE Data) Using Prepared Statements in PHP

In PHP, PDO (PHP Data Objects) can be used to securely interact with a MySQL database. Prepared statements ensure user input is handled safely by separating the SQL logic from the data, thus preventing SQL injection attacks where malicious SQL code might be inserted into user inputs. This is especially important when deleting data, as it ensures that user input is safely passed into the query. Before proceeding, ensure you have the db-connect.php file created, which will handle the database connection.

Create db-connect.php

To establish a connection to your MySQL database, create a

db-connect.php file. This file will use PDO to securely handle the interaction with the database:

```php
<?php

// Database connection details
$host = 'localhost';
$dbname = 'YourDatabaseName';  // Replace with your database name
$username = 'YourUserName';    // Replace with your database username
$password = 'YourPassword';    // Replace with your database password

try {
    // Create a new PDO instance
    $pdo = new PDO("mysql:host=$host;dbname=$dbname", $username, $password);

    // Set PDO to throw exceptions in case of errors
    $pdo->setAttribute(PDO::ATTR_ERRMODE, PDO::ERRMODE_EXCEPTION);

    echo "Connected successfully!";
} catch (PDOException $e) {
    // Handle connection errors
    echo "Connection failed: " . $e->getMessage();
```

```
}
?>
```

Save the file as db-connect.php.

Create delete-data.php

In this example, we demonstrate how to securely delete data from your database using prepared statements in PHP.

```php
<?php

// Include the database connection script
include("db-connect.php");

try {
    // Prepare the SQL DELETE statement with a placeholder for the
record ID
    $stmt = $pdo->prepare("DELETE FROM Test_Table WHERE id =
:record_id");

    // Bind the actual data to the placeholder
    $stmt->bindParam(':record_id', $record_id, PDO::PARAM_INT);

    // Example value for the record ID to delete (you would use
    // user input in a real scenario)
    $record_id = 1;

    // Execute the prepared statement
    $stmt->execute();

    echo "Data deleted successfully!";
} catch (PDOException $e) {
    echo "Error: " . $e->getMessage();
}

?>
```

Save the file as delete-data.php.

Breakdown of the Code

Database Connection:

The script starts by including the db-connect.php file, which contains the database connection details and establishes a PDO connection to the MySQL database.

Prepare the SQL Statement:

The SQL DELETE statement is prepared with a placeholder :record_id. This placeholder is where the actual ID of the record to be deleted will be inserted.

Bind Parameters:

The $stmt->bindParam() function binds the value of $record_id to the placeholder :record_id. This ensures the data is safely passed into the SQL statement, preventing SQL injection attacks.

Execute the Statement:

The prepared statement is executed with $stmt->execute(), which performs the actual deletion of the record from the database.

Result:

If the statement executes successfully, the message "Data deleted successfully!" is displayed. If any errors occur during the process, they are caught and displayed as an error message.

How to Run the Script

Open your browser and visit:

http://localhost/delete-data.php

This will execute the PHP script, connect to the MySQL database, and delete the record from the Test_Table where the id matches the record_id.

Delete (DELETE Data) Using Prepared Statements in Java

Deleting data from a database securely using prepared statements in Java is crucial for preventing SQL injection attacks and improving the performance of SQL operations. By using a PreparedStatement, user input is bound to the SQL query as parameters, ensuring that input is treated as data rather than executable code. Prepared statements also allow the database to pre-compile the SQL query, making it reusable for multiple executions and enhancing performance.

In this example, we will separate the database connection logic into a DBConnect.java file, and the delete operation will be handled in the main PdoDelete.java class.

Create DBConnect.java

First, create the **DBConnect.java** file to handle the connection to the MySQL database:

```java
import java.sql.Connection;
import java.sql.DriverManager;
import java.sql.SQLException;

public class DBConnect {

    // Method to establish a connection to the database
    public static Connection getConnection() {
        String url = "jdbc:mysql://localhost:3306/YourDatabaseName";
        // Replace above with your database URL

        String user = "YourUserName";
        // Replace above with your database username

        String password = "YourPassword";
        // Replace above with your database password

        Connection con = null;

        try {
            // Establish the connection to the database
            con = DriverManager.getConnection(url, user, password);
        } catch (SQLException e) {
            System.out.println("Connection failed: " + e.getMessage());
        }
        return con;
```

```
    }
}
```

Save the file as DBConnect.java.

Create PdoDelete.java

Next, create the **PdoDelete.java** text file, which imports the DBConnect class and deletes data from the database using a prepared statement:

```java
import java.sql.*;

public class PdoDelete {
    public static void main(String[] args) {

        // Connection object and PreparedStatement
        Connection con = null;
        PreparedStatement stmt = null;

        try {
            // Use the DBConnect class to establish the connection
            con = DBConnect.getConnection();

            if (con != null) {
                // Prepare the SQL DELETE statement with a placeholder
                String sql = "DELETE FROM Test_Table WHERE id = ?";
                stmt = con.prepareStatement(sql);

                // Set the value for the placeholder
                stmt.setInt(1, 1);  // ID of the record to delete

                // Execute the delete statement
                int rowsAffected = stmt.executeUpdate();

                if (rowsAffected > 0) {
                    System.out.println("Data deleted successfully!");
                } else {
                    System.out.println("No record found with the specified
id.");
```

```
        }
      } else {
          System.out.println("Failed to establish connection.");
      }

    } catch (SQLException e) {
        System.out.println("Error during SQL operation: " +
e.getMessage());

    } finally {
      // Close resources
      try {
          if (stmt != null) stmt.close();
          if (con != null) con.close();
      } catch (SQLException se) {
          System.out.println("Error closing resources: " +
se.getMessage());
      }
    }
  }
}
```

Save the file as PdoDelete.java.

Explanation

DBConnect.java:

Functionality: This class handles the database connection logic. The static method getConnection() establishes and returns a Connection object to interact with the MySQL database.

Customization: The connection parameters (URL, username, password) are hardcoded for simplicity. These can be customized to read from configuration files or environment variables for better flexibility.

PdoDelete.java:

Functionality: This class connects to the database using DBConnect.getConnection(), prepares an SQL DELETE statement with a placeholder for the id, binds the value to the placeholder, and executes the statement.

Error Handling: The code includes error handling to catch and display any SQL exceptions that might occur during the operation.

Resource Management: The finally block ensures that the PreparedStatement and Connection resources are closed after the operation is complete.

How to Compile and Run

Compile the classes:

javac DBConnect.java PdoDelete.java

Run the main class:

java PdoDelete

This will execute the PdoDelete class, which will connect to the database and delete the record from Test_Table where the id matches 1.

Chapter 5: Fetching Data with PDO

PDO (PHP Data Objects) is a database access library in PHP that provides a uniform method of interacting with different database management systems (DBMS). It allows you to fetch data from your database in a secure and efficient manner. Below, I'll cover the basics of fetching data with PDO, including how to prepare and execute queries, and the different methods of retrieving data.

Setting Up PDO Connection

Before fetching any data, you first need to establish a connection to your database using PDO.

Here's an example of how to connect to a MySQL database using PHP:

```php
<?php
$dsn = 'mysql:host=localhost;dbname=your_database';
$username = 'your_username';
$password = 'your_password';

try {
    $pdo = new PDO($dsn, $username, $password);
    // Set the PDO error mode to exception
```

```php
    $pdo->setAttribute(PDO::ATTR_ERRMODE,
PDO::ERRMODE_EXCEPTION);

    echo "Connected successfully";

} catch (PDOException $e) {

    echo "Connection failed: " . $e->getMessage();

}
?>
```

Here's an example of how to connect to a MySQL database using Java with the JDBC (Java Database Connectivity) API:

Add MySQL JDBC Driver

First, ensure that you have the MySQL JDBC driver (e.g., mysql-connector-java) in your project. If you're using Maven, you can add this dependency to your pom.xml:

```xml
<dependency>

    <groupId>mysql</groupId>

    <artifactId>mysql-connector-java</artifactId>

    <version>8.0.32</version> <!-- Use appropriate version -->

</dependency>
```

If you're not using Maven, you can manually download the JDBC driver from MySQL's website and add it to your project's classpath.

Java Code to Connect to MySQL

Here's the basic Java code to establish a connection to a

MySQL database:

```java
import java.sql.Connection;
import java.sql.DriverManager;
import java.sql.SQLException;

public class MySQLConnectionExample {
    public static void main(String[] args) {
        // MySQL database credentials
        String url = "jdbc:mysql://localhost:3306/your_database";
        // Database URL above

        String username = "your_username"; // Database username
        String password = "your_password"; // Database password

        // Establish the connection
        try {
            // Load the MySQL JDBC driver (optional in newer versions
            // of Java)
            Class.forName("com.mysql.cj.jdbc.Driver");

            // Open a connection
            Connection conn = DriverManager.getConnection(url,
username, password);

            // If connected successfully
            if (conn != null) {
                System.out.println("Connected to the database
successfully!");

            }

            // Close the connection
            conn.close();
        } catch (SQLException e) {
            System.err.println("SQL Exception: " + e.getMessage());
        } catch (ClassNotFoundException e) {
            System.err.println("JDBC Driver not found: " +
e.getMessage());
        }
    }
}
```

Fetching Data with PDO using PHP

There are several methods available for fetching data from the database with PDO, and the choice depends on how you want to handle the result set. The common methods are:

fetch() - Retrieves a single row from the result set.

fetchAll() - Retrieves all rows from the result set.

fetchColumn() - Fetches a single column value.

Using fetch() to Retrieve One Row with PHP

If you want to retrieve a single row from your query result, you can use the fetch() method. This method fetches the next row of the result set as an associative array, a numerical array, or both.

```php
<?php

$stmt = $pdo->query("SELECT id, name, email FROM users LIMIT 1");

$row = $stmt->fetch(PDO::FETCH_ASSOC);
// Above: Fetch a single row as an associative array

if ($row) {
    echo "ID: " . $row['id'] . "<br>";
    echo "Name: " . $row['name'] . "<br>";
```

```php
    echo "Email: " . $row['email'] . "<br>";
} else {
    echo "No records found.";
}

?>
```

Using fetchAll() to Retrieve All Rows using PHP

If you want to fetch all rows returned by the query, use the fetchAll() method. This will return an array of all rows as associative arrays.

```php
<?php

$stmt = $pdo->query("SELECT id, name, email FROM users");

$rows = $stmt->fetchAll(PDO::FETCH_ASSOC);
// Above: Fetch all rows as associative arrays

foreach ($rows as $row) {
    echo "ID: " . $row['id'] . "<br>";
    echo "Name: " . $row['name'] . "<br>";
    echo "Email: " . $row['email'] . "<br><br>";
}

?>
```

Using fetchColumn() to Retrieve a Single Value using PHP

If you're interested in retrieving a single column value (e.g.,

the value of a specific field), you can use the fetchColumn()
method. This is useful for situations where you want to fetch
one column's value from the first row of the result set.

```php
<?php

$stmt = $pdo->query("SELECT COUNT(*) FROM users");

$count = $stmt->fetchColumn();
// Above: Fetch the first column of the first row

echo "Total users: " . $count;

?>
```

Using Prepared Statements to Fetch Data using PHP

For added security (to avoid SQL injection), it's
recommended to use prepared statements when fetching
data with PDO. Here's an example of how to fetch data using
prepared statements with bound parameters:

```php
<?php

$id = 1;
$stmt = $pdo->prepare("SELECT id, name, email FROM users
WHERE id = :id");

$stmt->bindParam(':id', $id, PDO::PARAM_INT);
$stmt->execute();
```

```php
$row = $stmt->fetch(PDO::FETCH_ASSOC);
if ($row) {
    echo "ID: " . $row['id'] . "<br>";
    echo "Name: " . $row['name'] . "<br>";
    echo "Email: " . $row['email'] . "<br>";
} else {
    echo "No user found.";
}

?>
```

Fetching Data Efficiently using PHP

PDO is efficient, but in large datasets, fetching too many rows at once can consume too much memory. You can fetch data in chunks (e.g., 10 rows at a time) to optimize memory usage by using the fetch() method in a loop.

```php
<?php

$stmt = $pdo->query("SELECT id, name, email FROM users");
while ($row = $stmt->fetch(PDO::FETCH_ASSOC)) {
    echo "ID: " . $row['id'] . "<br>";
    echo "Name: " . $row['name'] . "<br>";
    echo "Email: " . $row['email'] . "<br><br>";
}

?>
```

Error Handling and Exception Management using PHP

When fetching data with PDO, it is important to handle potential errors gracefully. PDO allows you to configure error handling with setAttribute(). The most common error mode is PDO::ERRMODE_EXCEPTION, which throws exceptions on errors.

```php
<?php

try {
    $stmt = $pdo->query("SELECT id, name, email FROM users");
    while ($row = $stmt->fetch(PDO::FETCH_ASSOC)) {
        echo "ID: " . $row['id'] . "<br>";
        echo "Name: " . $row['name'] . "<br>";
        echo "Email: " . $row['email'] . "<br><br>";
    }
} catch (PDOException $e) {
    echo "Error: " . $e->getMessage();
}

?>
```

Fetching Data Efficiently with PHP

When working with databases, especially large datasets, fetching data efficiently is crucial to optimize performance, reduce memory consumption, and improve the user experience. PHP offers several techniques to fetch data efficiently from a database. In this guide, we will explore various strategies for fetching data with PHP, including using PDO (PHP Data Objects), managing memory usage, handling large datasets, and ensuring that your application remains responsive even with massive amounts of data.

Why Efficient Data Fetching Matters

Memory Usage:

Fetching a large result set all at once can cause excessive memory usage, which might result in slow performance or memory overflow. Efficiently fetching and processing data reduces memory consumption and allows the application to scale.

Performance:

Querying a database can be slow, especially if you're dealing with complex joins or large tables. By fetching data incrementally or using optimized queries, you can reduce query times and improve overall performance.

User Experience:

Fetching data efficiently allows your application to return results faster, leading to a smoother and more responsive user experience. This is especially important in real-time applications or web apps where speed is crucial.

Techniques for Fetching Data Efficiently in PHP

Using PDO for Database Interaction

The PHP Data Objects (PDO) extension provides a consistent and efficient way to interact with databases. It supports multiple database systems, including MySQL, PostgreSQL,

SQLite, and others. PDO also offers several methods for fetching data, each suited for different scenarios.

Fetching One Row at a Time with fetch()

When dealing with large datasets, it's often best to fetch data one row at a time. This method allows your script to process each row as it's retrieved, avoiding the need to load the entire result set into memory at once.

Here's an example of how to fetch a single row at a time using PDO:

```php
<?php

$pdo = new PDO('mysql:host=localhost;dbname=your_database',
'username', 'password');

$query = "SELECT id, name, email FROM users";
$stmt = $pdo->query($query);

while ($row = $stmt->fetch(PDO::FETCH_ASSOC)) {
    echo "ID: " . $row['id'] . "<br>";
    echo "Name: " . $row['name'] . "<br>";
    echo "Email: " . $row['email'] . "<br><br>";
}
```

```
?>
```

In this example:

fetch(PDO::FETCH_ASSOC) retrieves each row as an associative array, one at a time.

The while loop ensures that you only process one row at a time, which keeps memory usage low.

Why This is Efficient:

Memory Usage: Only one row is in memory at any given time, minimizing memory consumption.

Performance: This method allows your script to process and output data immediately without waiting for the entire result set to be loaded.

Scalability: It scales well even with large datasets, such as thousands or millions of records.

Using fetchAll() for Small Result Sets

If you expect a relatively small number of rows to be returned by your query, you can use the fetchAll() method to retrieve all rows at once. This method returns the entire result set as an array, which can be useful when the dataset is manageable and you want to perform operations on all the rows at once.


```php
<?php

$pdo = new PDO('mysql:host=localhost;dbname=your_database',
'username', 'password');
```

```php
$query = "SELECT id, name, email FROM users";
$stmt = $pdo->query($query);

$rows = $stmt->fetchAll(PDO::FETCH_ASSOC);
// Above: Fetch all rows at once

foreach ($rows as $row) {
    echo "ID: " . $row['id'] . "<br>";
    echo "Name: " . $row['name'] . "<br>";
    echo "Email: " . $row['email'] . "<br><br>";
}

?>
```

Why This is Efficient:

Simple and Fast: When the result set is small, fetching all rows at once is faster and simpler, as you don't need to loop through and fetch rows individually.

Use Cases: This method is best used for result sets that are small enough to be processed in memory, like queries that return a few hundred or thousand rows.

Using fetchColumn() for Single Values

If you only need to fetch a single column value (e.g., counting rows or retrieving a specific value), fetchColumn() is a great way to fetch just that value efficiently. This is often used when performing aggregate operations or retrieving a single field from the first row of the result set.

```php
<?php

$pdo = new PDO('mysql:host=localhost;dbname=your_database',
'username', 'password');

$query = "SELECT COUNT(*) FROM users";
$stmt = $pdo->query($query);

$count = $stmt->fetchColumn();
// Above: Fetch the first column of the first row

echo "Total users: " . $count;

?>
```

Why This is Efficient:

Minimal Resource Usage: Fetching a single value directly without loading the entire result set reduces overhead.

Quick Access: If you're only interested in one value (e.g., total count, maximum value), fetchColumn() is the most efficient way to retrieve it.

Using Prepared Statements for Secure Fetching

To improve security, particularly against SQL injection, it's essential to use prepared statements with bound parameters. Here's an example of how to fetch data using a prepared statement:

```php
<?php

$pdo = new PDO('mysql:host=localhost;dbname=your_database',
'username', 'password');

// Using a prepared statement to fetch data securely
$query = "SELECT id, name, email FROM users WHERE id = :id";
$stmt = $pdo->prepare($query);

$stmt->bindParam(':id', $id, PDO::PARAM_INT);
$id = 1; // Example of user ID to fetch
$stmt->execute();

$row = $stmt->fetch(PDO::FETCH_ASSOC);
if ($row) {
    echo "ID: " . $row['id'] . "<br>";
    echo "Name: " . $row['name'] . "<br>";
    echo "Email: " . $row['email'] . "<br>";
} else {
    echo "No user found.";
}

?>
```

Why This is Efficient:

Security: Prepared statements protect against SQL injection by separating SQL code from data.

Reusability: Prepared statements can be reused with different parameters, improving performance when executing similar queries multiple times.

Handling Large Result Sets Efficiently

For very large result sets, you may want to fetch the data in smaller chunks rather than all at once. This method is often referred to as batch processing or pagination. It involves limiting the number of rows retrieved per query and processing them in steps.

```php
<?php

$pdo = new PDO('mysql:host=localhost;dbname=your_database',
'username', 'password');

$limit = 100; // Number of rows per batch
$offset = 0;

do {
    $query = "SELECT id, name, email FROM users LIMIT $limit
OFFSET $offset";

    $stmt = $pdo->query($query);
    $rows = $stmt->fetchAll(PDO::FETCH_ASSOC);

    foreach ($rows as $row) {
        echo "ID: " . $row['id'] . "<br>";
        echo "Name: " . $row['name'] . "<br>";
        echo "Email: " . $row['email'] . "<br><br>";
    }

    $offset += $limit; // Move to the next batch
} while (count($rows) > 0);

?>
```

Fetching Data with PDO using Java

In Java, you'll typically use Statement or PreparedStatement to execute a query. After that, you can use the ResultSet to fetch data. Here are examples corresponding to the different methods for fetching data.

Using Statement to Retrieve One Row using Java

To retrieve a single row of data, you can use ResultSet.next() to move through the result set. The ResultSet.getString() method retrieves values by column name or index.

```java
import java.sql.*;

public class FetchOneRow {
    public static void main(String[] args) {
        String url = "jdbc:mysql://localhost:3306/your_database";
        String username = "your_username";
        String password = "your_password";

        try (Connection conn = DriverManager.getConnection(url,
username, password);

        Statement stmt = conn.createStatement()) {

        String query = "SELECT id, name, email FROM users
LIMIT 1";

        ResultSet rs = stmt.executeQuery(query);
```

```java
            if (rs.next()) {
                // Retrieve data from the first (and only) row
                int id = rs.getInt("id");
                String name = rs.getString("name");
                String email = rs.getString("email");

                // Display the data
                System.out.println("ID: " + id);
                System.out.println("Name: " + name);
                System.out.println("Email: " + email);
            } else {
                System.out.println("No records found.");
            }

        } catch (SQLException e) {
            System.err.println("SQL Exception: " + e.getMessage());
        }
    }
}
```

Using Statement to Retrieve All Rows using Java

If you want to retrieve all rows from a query, you can iterate through the ResultSet using a while loop.

```java
import java.sql.*;

public class FetchAllRows {
    public static void main(String[] args) {
        String url = "jdbc:mysql://localhost:3306/your_database";
        String username = "your_username";
        String password = "your_password";
```

```java
    try (Connection conn = DriverManager.getConnection(url,
username, password);

        Statement stmt = conn.createStatement()) {

        String query = "SELECT id, name, email FROM users";
        ResultSet rs = stmt.executeQuery(query);

        while (rs.next()) {
            int id = rs.getInt("id");
            String name = rs.getString("name");
            String email = rs.getString("email");

            // Display the data for each row
            System.out.println("ID: " + id);
            System.out.println("Name: " + name);
            System.out.println("Email: " + email);
            System.out.println();
        }

    } catch (SQLException e) {
        System.err.println("SQL Exception: " + e.getMessage());
    }
  }
}
```

Using PreparedStatement to Fetch Data with Parameters using Java

For security reasons, it's recommended to use PreparedStatement to prevent SQL injection. Here's an example where we fetch data based on a dynamic parameter (e.g., a user ID).

```java
import java.sql.*;

public class FetchWithPreparedStatement {
    public static void main(String[] args) {
        String url = "jdbc:mysql://localhost:3306/your_database";
        String username = "your_username";
        String password = "your_password";

        try (Connection conn = DriverManager.getConnection(url,
username, password)) {

            String query = "SELECT id, name, email FROM users
WHERE id = ?";

            try (PreparedStatement pstmt =
conn.prepareStatement(query)) {

                pstmt.setInt(1, 1); // Set the ID parameter (e.g., 1)

                ResultSet rs = pstmt.executeQuery();

                if (rs.next()) {
                    int id = rs.getInt("id");
                    String name = rs.getString("name");
                    String email = rs.getString("email");

                    // Display the data
                    System.out.println("ID: " + id);
                    System.out.println("Name: " + name);
                    System.out.println("Email: " + email);
                } else {
                    System.out.println("No user found.");
                }

            }

        } catch (SQLException e) {
            System.err.println("SQL Exception: " + e.getMessage());
        }
    }
}
```

Fetching a Single Value (Similar to fetchColumn() in PDO) using Java

If you only need to retrieve a single value (like a count or sum), you can use ResultSet.getInt() or ResultSet.getString() depending on the data type.

```java
import java.sql.*;

public class FetchSingleValue {
    public static void main(String[] args) {
        String url = "jdbc:mysql://localhost:3306/your_database";
        String username = "your_username";
        String password = "your_password";

        try (Connection conn = DriverManager.getConnection(url, username, password);

            Statement stmt = conn.createStatement()) {

            String query = "SELECT COUNT(*) FROM users";
            ResultSet rs = stmt.executeQuery(query);

            if (rs.next()) {
                int count = rs.getInt(1);
                // Above: Retrieve the first column of the first row

                System.out.println("Total users: " + count);
            }
        } catch (SQLException e) {
            System.err.println("SQL Exception: " + e.getMessage());
        }
    }
}
```

Error Handling and Exception Management using Java

Just like with PDO, it's important to handle exceptions that may arise during database operations. The most common approach is to use try-catch blocks to catch SQLException.

```java
import java.sql.*;

public class FetchWithErrorHandling {
    public static void main(String[] args) {
        String url = "jdbc:mysql://localhost:3306/your_database";
        String username = "your_username";
        String password = "your_password";

        try (Connection conn = DriverManager.getConnection(url, username, password);

            Statement stmt = conn.createStatement()) {

            String query = "SELECT id, name, email FROM users";
            ResultSet rs = stmt.executeQuery(query);

            while (rs.next()) {
                int id = rs.getInt("id");
                String name = rs.getString("name");
                String email = rs.getString("email");

                // Display data
                System.out.println("ID: " + id);
                System.out.println("Name: " + name);
                System.out.println("Email: " + email);
                System.out.println();
            }

        } catch (SQLException e) {
            System.err.println("SQL Exception: " + e.getMessage());
        }
    }
}
```

```
}
```

Fetching Data Efficiently with Java

When dealing with large datasets in database queries, fetching all rows at once can be inefficient and resource-intensive. If you're processing thousands or millions of rows, loading the entire result set into memory at once can significantly slow down your application or even cause memory overflow issues. To handle large datasets more efficiently, it's a better practice to process the data one row

at a time, which is typically done using a cursor-based approach, where you fetch each row sequentially as needed.

Why Fetching Rows One by One Is Efficient

Memory Usage:

When you fetch all rows at once using methods like fetchAll(), the entire result set is loaded into memory as an array or list. If you have a large number of records, this can lead to excessive memory consumption, especially on machines with limited RAM. By fetching rows one at a time, only a single row is stored in memory at any given moment, reducing the memory footprint of your application.

Performance:
Fetching large datasets in chunks or one by one allows your application to start processing the results immediately, without waiting for the entire dataset to be fetched into memory. This can be especially beneficial when you need to display data to users incrementally or perform operations like writing the data to disk or sending it over a network.

Database Load:

Many database management systems (DBMS) are optimized to handle row-by-row fetching efficiently. Databases are designed to serve data sequentially, so fetching rows one by

one doesn't overload the system with unnecessary queries or excessive data retrieval.

Scalability:
As your dataset grows, a method that fetches one row at a time scales much better than fetching all rows at once. Even when working with very large tables, this approach remains efficient and can handle datasets that exceed the available memory.

How to Fetch Rows One by One in Java:

In Java, you can achieve this by using a while loop along with the ResultSet.next() method. This method moves the cursor to the next row in the result set, and if there is a row, it returns true, allowing you to fetch the data for that row. Once all rows are processed, ResultSet.next() returns false, signaling that there are no more rows to retrieve.

Example of Fetching Rows One by One in Java:

```java
import java.sql.*;

public class EfficientRowFetching {
    public static void main(String[] args) {
        String url = "jdbc:mysql://localhost:3306/your_database";
        String username = "your_username";
        String password = "your_password";

        try (Connection conn = DriverManager.getConnection(url,
username, password);

            Statement stmt = conn.createStatement()) {

            String query = "SELECT id, name, email FROM users";
            ResultSet rs = stmt.executeQuery(query);

            // Fetch and process each row one by one
            while (rs.next()) {
                int id = rs.getInt("id");
                String name = rs.getString("name");
                String email = rs.getString("email");

                // Process data (e.g., display or write to a file)
                System.out.println("ID: " + id);
                System.out.println("Name: " + name);
                System.out.println("Email: " + email);
                System.out.println();
            }

        } catch (SQLException e) {
            System.err.println("SQL Exception: " + e.getMessage());
        }
    }
}
```

Chapter 6: Working with Transactions in PDO

In database-driven applications, it's essential to ensure that a series of database operations execute as a single unit, so that the database remains in a consistent state. A transaction allows you to group multiple operations together, ensuring that all of them succeed or none of them are applied. This is crucial when performing operations such as transferring money between accounts, or updating multiple tables simultaneously, where partial updates could lead to data corruption or inconsistency.

PHP's PDO (PHP Data Objects) extension provides built-in support for handling transactions in a safe and efficient manner. In this guide, we'll explore how to use PDO to manage database transactions, ensuring data integrity and error handling during complex operations.

In Java, managing database transactions is a critical aspect of ensuring data integrity and consistency, especially when multiple operations must succeed or fail together. Java provides built-in support for handling database transactions through the JDBC (Java Database Connectivity) API, which allows developers to interact with databases efficiently. Just like PHP's PDO (PHP Data Objects) extension, JDBC offers a way to group multiple SQL operations into a single transaction, ensuring atomicity, consistency, isolation, and durability (ACID properties).

What Are Transactions?

A database transaction is a sequence of one or more operations (such as queries, updates, inserts, or deletes) that are executed as a single unit of work. The primary goal of a transaction is to ensure that a series of operations on a database are completed successfully, or if any part of the operation fails, the entire sequence of operations is undone to preserve the integrity of the data.

Transactions are fundamental in database management systems (DBMS) because they provide a mechanism to handle multiple operations that need to be treated as a single, atomic operation. This is crucial in ensuring data integrity, consistency, and reliability when dealing with complex data manipulations in multi-user or distributed environments.

Importance of Transactions in Ensuring Data Integrity

A transaction must adhere to the ACID properties to ensure the integrity of the data. These ACID properties are the backbone of database transactions and are essential for maintaining data consistency even in the presence of system crashes, power failures, or concurrent access by multiple users.

Atomicity

Atomicity ensures that a transaction is treated as a single "unit of work," meaning that either all the operations within the transaction are completed successfully, or none of them are. If any operation within the transaction fails, the entire transaction is rolled back, and the database is restored to its previous state. This prevents partial updates from occurring, which could lead to inconsistent data.

Example: In a banking system, a transaction to transfer money from one account to another involves two operations:

Deducting the amount from the sender's account.

Adding the amount to the recipient's account.

If an error occurs during the second operation (e.g., the recipient's account cannot be updated), the first operation (deducting the money from the sender) is undone as well, ensuring that no money is lost or incorrectly transferred.

Consistency

Consistency ensures that a transaction brings the database from one valid state to another valid state, meaning that the data must always be valid according to the rules (such as constraints, triggers, etc.) of the database. If a transaction violates any integrity constraints, such as a foreign key constraint or a unique constraint, it will be rolled back.

Example: In a library system, a transaction that involves borrowing a book will not only update the borrower's information but also check that the book exists and is available. If any inconsistency arises (e.g., trying to borrow a book that's already checked out), the transaction will fail,

and the database will not be updated.

Isolation

Isolation ensures that transactions are executed in such a way that their intermediate states are not visible to other transactions. This is particularly important in multi-user environments where multiple transactions can be executed concurrently. The database guarantees that each transaction will appear to execute in isolation, even if they run simultaneously. Different isolation levels (such as Read Uncommitted, Read Committed, Repeatable Read, and Serializable) define the level of visibility that one transaction has over another.

Example: Consider two transactions:

Transaction A transfers money from Account X to Account Y.

Transaction B reads the balance of Account X.

If Transaction A has not yet committed its changes but Transaction B reads the old balance, this could result in inconsistent or incorrect data being displayed. Isolation ensures that either Transaction A fully completes (and its effects are visible to Transaction B) or Transaction B sees the state of the database as it was before Transaction A started.

Durability

Durability guarantees that once a transaction has been committed, the changes are permanent, even in the event of a system failure (such as a power outage). Once a transaction is successfully committed, the data will not be lost or reverted, even if the system crashes immediately afterward. This is typically achieved through the use of transaction logs and backups.

Example: In an e-commerce system, when a user completes a purchase, the transaction that records the order is committed to the database. Even if the system crashes right after the commit, the purchase data is saved and can be recovered, ensuring that no orders are lost.

Real-World Examples of Transactions

Banking Systems

Banking applications rely heavily on transactions. For example, transferring money between two bank accounts requires multiple steps:

Deducting money from one account.

Adding money to another account.

Both of these operations must succeed or fail together to maintain accurate financial records. If the system fails after the first operation but before the second operation completes, a rollback ensures that the deduction is undone, preventing data corruption or fraud.

Online Shopping

In an online shopping platform, a user's shopping cart, payment information, and order details are typically handled as a single transaction. If the payment is processed successfully, the order is placed, and inventory is updated. However, if the payment fails, the transaction is rolled back, and the inventory is not affected. This guarantees that users can never place an order without the transaction being fully successful.

Inventory Management Systems

Inventory management systems use transactions to ensure that stock quantities are accurately updated. When an item is sold, its quantity must be deducted from the inventory database. A transaction ensures that this update is done atomically, so if there's an error during the process (e.g., the database is unavailable), the system won't mistakenly deduct inventory without completing the sale.

Using Transactions with PDO

Database transactions are crucial for maintaining data integrity when performing multiple operations that need to be treated as a single unit. In PHP, PDO (PHP Data Objects) provides a simple and efficient way to manage transactions. This guide will walk you through how to start, commit, and roll back transactions using PDO, ensuring that your data remains consistent even in the event of an error.

Starting a Transaction using PHP

To begin a transaction in PDO, you use the beginTransaction() method. This method tells the database that a series of operations will be performed as a single transaction. From the moment you call beginTransaction(), no changes are committed to the database until the transaction is either committed or rolled back.

Example Code

```php
<?php

// Create a new PDO instance
$pdo = new PDO('mysql:host=localhost;dbname=testdb', 'username', 'password');

// Set PDO error mode to exception
$pdo->setAttribute(PDO::ATTR_ERRMODE, PDO::ERRMODE_EXCEPTION);

// Start the transaction
$pdo->beginTransaction();

try {
    // Perform your database operations
    $pdo->exec("INSERT INTO users (name, email) VALUES ('John Doe', 'john@example.com')");

    $pdo->exec("UPDATE accounts SET balance = balance - 100 WHERE user_id = 1");

    // If everything is successful, commit the transaction
    $pdo->commit();
    echo "Transaction successfully completed!";
} catch (PDOException $e) {
    // In case of an error, roll back the transaction
    $pdo->rollBack();
```

```
    echo "Failed to complete transaction: " . $e->getMessage();
}

?>
```

Starting a Transaction using Java

To begin a transaction in JDBC, you need to disable auto-commit mode by calling setAutoCommit(false) on your Connection object. This tells the database that you will perform a series of operations as part of a single transaction. From the moment you call setAutoCommit(false), no changes are committed to the database until you explicitly commit or roll back the transaction.

Example Code

```
import java.sql.*;

public class DatabaseTransactionExample {
    public static void main(String[] args) {
        Connection connection = null;
        PreparedStatement stmt1 = null;
        PreparedStatement stmt2 = null;

        try {
            // Establish connection to the database
            connection =
DriverManager.getConnection("jdbc:mysql://localhost:3306/testdb",
"username", "password");
```

```java
        // Disable auto-commit mode to begin the transaction
        connection.setAutoCommit(false);

        // First operation: Insert a new user
        String sql1 = "INSERT INTO users (name, email) VALUES
(?, ?)";

        stmt1 = connection.prepareStatement(sql1);
        stmt1.setString(1, "John Doe");
        stmt1.setString(2, "john@example.com");
        stmt1.executeUpdate();

        // Second operation: Update the user's account balance
        String sql2 = "UPDATE accounts SET balance = balance - ?
WHERE user_id = ?";

        stmt2 = connection.prepareStatement(sql2);
        stmt2.setInt(1, 100);
        stmt2.setInt(2, 1);
        stmt2.executeUpdate();

        // If everything is successful, commit the transaction
        connection.commit();
        System.out.println("Transaction successfully completed!");

    } catch (SQLException e) {
        try {
            // In case of an error, roll back the transaction
            if (connection != null) {
                connection.rollback();
                System.out.println("Transaction rolled back due to an
error.");

            }
        } catch (SQLException rollbackEx) {
            System.out.println("Error rolling back transaction: " +
rollbackEx.getMessage());

        }
        System.out.println("Error: " + e.getMessage());
    } finally {
        try {
            // Reset auto-commit mode and close resources
            if (connection != null) {
```

```
            connection.setAutoCommit(true);
        }
        if (stmt1 != null) stmt1.close();
        if (stmt2 != null) stmt2.close();
        if (connection != null) connection.close();
      } catch (SQLException e) {
        System.out.println("Error closing resources: " +
e.getMessage());
      }
    }
  }
}
```

Committing a Transaction

Once you have performed all the operations within a transaction and everything is successful, you need to call the commit() method to save all changes to the database. The commit() method will make all the changes permanent.

In the example above, the transaction is committed by calling $pdo->commit() if all the operations (like inserting a new user and updating an account balance) are successful.

If the transaction is successful, the changes are saved to the database. Without committing the transaction, the database would not know that the operations should be finalized.

Rolling Back a Transaction

If an error occurs during the transaction (such as a failed query or an exception), you can use the rollBack() method to

undo all the operations that were performed since the transaction began. This ensures that the database is returned to its state before the transaction started, preserving data integrity.

In the example above, the catch block handles any exceptions that might occur during the transaction. If an exception is thrown, the rollBack() method is called to revert the changes made during the transaction.

Why Use Transactions?

Transactions are essential when performing multiple operations that depend on each other. For example, in an e-commerce site, when a user makes a purchase, the following operations may occur:

Deduct money from the user's account.

Update the stock quantity of an item.

Insert a record into the orders table.

Each of these operations must succeed together. If one fails, all changes must be rolled back to ensure that the database remains in a consistent state. Without transactions, an error

in the middle of the process could lead to inconsistent or corrupt data (e.g., money being deducted but stock not being updated).

Chapter 7: Advanced SQL Queries with PDO

Advanced SQL queries in both Java and PHP can be efficiently handled using their respective database interaction tools: JDBC (Java Database Connectivity) for Java and PDO (PHP Data Objects) for PHP. Both JDBC and PDO allow developers to perform complex database operations securely by supporting prepared statements and parameterized queries, which protect against SQL injection. Advanced SQL techniques such as joining multiple tables, using subqueries, applying aggregate functions, and managing transactions can be executed with ease in both languages. With JDBC in Java, you can manage these queries using SQL statements and ResultSet objects, while PDO in PHP provides similar functionality with fetch methods. Both approaches support various database systems, allowing developers to write database-agnostic code. By leveraging advanced SQL features like pagination, grouping, and sorting, JDBC and PDO enable robust data manipulation and retrieval in modern web applications.

Working with Joins

Joins are essential when you need to retrieve related data from multiple tables. Both PHP (using PDO) and Java (using JDBC) support executing advanced queries with different types of joins like INNER JOIN, LEFT JOIN, and RIGHT JOIN.

PHP (PDO) Example:

```php
// Create a PDO connection
$pdo = new PDO('mysql:host=localhost;dbname=testdb', 'username',
'password');

$pdo->setAttribute(PDO::ATTR_ERRMODE,
PDO::ERRMODE_EXCEPTION);

// SQL with INNER JOIN
$sql = "SELECT users.name, orders.order_date
     FROM users
     INNER JOIN orders ON users.id = orders.user_id";
$stmt = $pdo->prepare($sql);
$stmt->execute();
$results = $stmt->fetchAll(PDO::FETCH_ASSOC);

foreach ($results as $row) {
   echo "Name: " . $row['name'] . ", Order Date: " . $row['order_date'] .
"<br>";

}
```

In this example, an INNER JOIN retrieves users and their related orders. You can similarly use LEFT JOIN and RIGHT JOIN.

```php
// LEFT JOIN example

$sql = "SELECT users.name, orders.order_date
     FROM users
     LEFT JOIN orders ON users.id = orders.user_id";
```

Java (JDBC) Example:

```java
// JDBC Connection
```

```java
Connection conn =
DriverManager.getConnection("jdbc:mysql://localhost:3306/testdb",
"username", "password");

// SQL with INNER JOIN
String sql = "SELECT users.name, orders.order_date " +
        "FROM users " +
        "INNER JOIN orders ON users.id = orders.user_id";
PreparedStatement stmt = conn.prepareStatement(sql);

ResultSet rs = stmt.executeQuery();

while (rs.next()) {
    String name = rs.getString("name");
    Date orderDate = rs.getDate("order_date");
    System.out.println("Name: " + name + ", Order Date: " +
orderDate);

}

// Close the connection
rs.close();
stmt.close();
conn.close();
```

In the JDBC example, we use ResultSet to retrieve and print data from an INNER JOIN. You can switch to LEFT JOIN or RIGHT JOIN by adjusting the SQL query.

Using Aggregates

Aggregates are useful for summarizing data. Functions like COUNT(), SUM(), AVG(), and MAX() are often used with GROUP BY to group records.

PHP (PDO) Example:

```php
// GROUP BY and COUNT example
$sql = "SELECT users.name, COUNT(orders.id) AS total_orders
     FROM users
     LEFT JOIN orders ON users.id = orders.user_id
     GROUP BY users.name
     HAVING total_orders > 0"; // Optionally filter with HAVING

$stmt = $pdo->prepare($sql);
$stmt->execute();
$results = $stmt->fetchAll(PDO::FETCH_ASSOC);

foreach ($results as $row) {
   echo "Name: " . $row['name'] . ", Total Orders: " .
$row['total_orders'] . "<br>";

}
```

This query counts the number of orders for each user and filters those who have placed at least one order using the HAVING clause.

Java (JDBC) Example:

```java
String sql = "SELECT users.name, COUNT(orders.id) AS total_orders " +

        "FROM users " +
        "LEFT JOIN orders ON users.id = orders.user_id " +
        "GROUP BY users.name " +
        "HAVING total_orders > 0";

PreparedStatement stmt = conn.prepareStatement(sql);
ResultSet rs = stmt.executeQuery();

while (rs.next()) {
    String name = rs.getString("name");
    int totalOrders = rs.getInt("total_orders");
    System.out.println("Name: " + name + ", Total Orders: " +
totalOrders);

}
```

In the JDBC example, we use GROUP BY and HAVING to count the total orders per user.

Subqueries

Subqueries allow you to nest queries within another SQL query. This is useful for filtering data based on results from other queries.

PHP (PDO) Example:

```php
// Subquery example
$sql = "SELECT name
        FROM users
        WHERE id IN (SELECT user_id FROM orders WHERE total >
100)";

$stmt = $pdo->prepare($sql);
$stmt->execute();
$results = $stmt->fetchAll(PDO::FETCH_ASSOC);

foreach ($results as $row) {
    echo "Name: " . $row['name'] . "<br>";
}
```

In this example, we use a subquery to select users who have placed orders with a total greater than 100.

Java (JDBC) Example:

```java
String sql = "SELECT name " +
             "FROM users " +
             "WHERE id IN (SELECT user_id FROM orders WHERE total
> 100)";

PreparedStatement stmt = conn.prepareStatement(sql);
ResultSet rs = stmt.executeQuery();

while (rs.next()) {
    String name = rs.getString("name");
    System.out.println("Name: " + name);
}
```

Chapter 8: Handling Errors with PDO

PHP's PDO (PHP Data Objects) provides a robust and flexible mechanism for handling database errors. By default, PDO offers several error handling modes, including silent, warning, and exception. The most commonly used mode is exception, which throws a PDOException when an error occurs, making it easier to catch and handle database issues.

To enable this mode, you can set the error handling attribute using:

```
$pdo->setAttribute(PDO::ATTR_ERRMODE,
PDO::ERRMODE_EXCEPTION);.
```

This approach allows developers to implement error-handling routines using try-catch blocks to gracefully manage failed queries, transaction errors, and connection issues. Properly handling errors ensures that your application can provide informative feedback and take corrective actions when necessary, which is crucial for maintaining data integrity and improving user experience.

Exception Mode: PDO Error Modes in PHP and Java

In PHP, PDO (PHP Data Objects) provides three different error handling modes to manage how errors are reported:

Silent Mode (PDO::ERRMODE_SILENT):

In silent mode, PDO fails silently without producing any error messages. You must manually check for errors using $pdo->errorInfo(). This mode is not ideal for development since it can make debugging more difficult.

```
$pdo->setAttribute(PDO::ATTR_ERRMODE,
PDO::ERRMODE_SILENT);
$stmt = $pdo->prepare("SELECT * FROM non_existent_table");
$stmt->execute();

if ($stmt->errorCode() != '00000') {
    echo "Error: " . implode(", ", $stmt->errorInfo());
}
```

Warning Mode (PDO::ERRMODE_WARNING):

This mode triggers a PHP warning when an error occurs. The script will continue execution, but warnings will be logged or displayed, making it somewhat easier to debug.

```
$pdo->setAttribute(PDO::ATTR_ERRMODE,
PDO::ERRMODE_WARNING);
$stmt = $pdo->prepare("SELECT * FROM non_existent_table");
$stmt->execute(); // Issues a warning but continues running
```

Exception Mode (PDO::ERRMODE_EXCEPTION):

Exception mode is the most recommended for error handling. When an error occurs, it throws a PDOException, which can be caught in a try-catch block. This makes it easier to handle errors gracefully and is ideal for development and production environments.

```
$pdo->setAttribute(PDO::ATTR_ERRMODE,
PDO::ERRMODE_EXCEPTION);

try {
    $stmt = $pdo->prepare("SELECT * FROM non_existent_table");
    $stmt->execute();
} catch (PDOException $e) {
    echo "Database error: " . $e->getMessage();
}
```

Exception Handling in Java

In Java, exceptions are handled using try-catch blocks, and SQL errors are typically caught using SQLException. While Java doesn't have the concept of different error modes like PDO in PHP, it provides a standard way to catch and handle exceptions thrown during database interactions.

```
import java.sql.*;

public class DatabaseExample {
    public static void main(String[] args) {
        Connection conn = null;
```

```java
try {
    // Connect to the database
    conn =
DriverManager.getConnection("jdbc:mysql://localhost/testdb", "root",
"password");

    // Perform a query
    Statement stmt = conn.createStatement();
    ResultSet rs = stmt.executeQuery("SELECT * FROM
non_existent_table");

} catch (SQLException e) {
    System.out.println("SQL Error: " + e.getMessage());
} finally {
    try {
        if (conn != null) conn.close();
    } catch (SQLException e) {
        System.out.println("Failed to close connection: " +
e.getMessage());

    }
  }
 }
}
```

Custom Error Handling with try-catch

Using try-catch blocks allows you to catch exceptions and handle them gracefully. This is especially useful in situations where you want to log errors, send notifications, or perform fallback operations.

PHP Example:

```php
try {
    $stmt = $pdo->prepare("INSERT INTO users (name, email)
VALUES ('John', 'john@example.com')");

    $stmt->execute();
    echo "User added successfully!";
} catch (PDOException $e) {
    echo "Failed to add user: " . $e->getMessage();
    // Additional custom error handling (e.g., logging or notifying)
}
```

Java Example:

```java
try {
    String query = "INSERT INTO users (name, email) VALUES
('John', 'john@example.com')";

    Statement stmt = conn.createStatement();
    stmt.executeUpdate(query);
    System.out.println("User added successfully!");
} catch (SQLException e) {
    System.out.println("Failed to add user: " + e.getMessage());
    // Custom error handling
}
```

Debugging Queries

Debugging database queries is essential for identifying issues during development. Both PHP and Java provide ways to inspect SQL queries before they are executed to identify syntax or logic errors.

PHP Debugging Example:

Use var_dump() or echo to print the query string before execution.

For prepared statements, you can inspect the bound parameters.

```
// Debugging a prepared statement
$stmt = $pdo->prepare("SELECT * FROM users WHERE id = :id");
$stmt->bindParam(':id', $id, PDO::PARAM_INT);
echo "SQL: " . $stmt->queryString;
$stmt->execute();
```

Java Debugging Example:

You can log the query string before execution, especially when using PreparedStatement:

```
PreparedStatement stmt = conn.prepareStatement("SELECT * FROM users WHERE id = ?");

stmt.setInt(1, 10);
System.out.println("SQL: SELECT * FROM users WHERE id = 10");
// Simulate the query being run above

ResultSet rs = stmt.executeQuery();
```

Debugging Tools

Both PHP and Java can benefit from debugging tools and techniques:

In PHP, tools like Xdebug can provide more insights into SQL errors by integrating with the development environment.

In Java, logging frameworks like Log4j or SLF4J can be used to log detailed query information and errors to help with

debugging.

By leveraging proper error modes, handling exceptions gracefully, and using debugging techniques, you can efficiently troubleshoot database issues and ensure your application handles errors robustly.

Chapter 9: Secure File Uploads with PDO

Secure file uploads are a critical aspect of web application security, and using PDO in PHP can help handle the database aspects of file uploads more securely. When uploading files, it's essential to validate the file type, size, and ensure that no malicious files are uploaded. PDO itself is not directly involved in the file upload process but is used to store file metadata (e.g., file name, path, size) securely in the database. Using prepared statements in PDO helps prevent SQL injection attacks by safely binding file data (like names or paths) to the database queries. Additionally, it's crucial to sanitize file names, store files in a secure location outside the web root, and use unique file names to avoid overwriting. Combined with proper server-side validation and PDO's secure querying, file uploads can be managed more securely, reducing the risk of security vulnerabilities in your web application.

Storing File Paths and Handling File Uploads Securely in PHP and Java

When dealing with file uploads, one of the key tasks is securely storing file paths in a database and managing potential file upload errors effectively. Below are examples of how to implement this in both PHP (using PDO) and Java.

Storing File Paths in PHP (Using PDO)

In PHP, you can use PDO to securely store file paths in your database. Here's a simple example of how to handle a file upload and store the file path securely:

```php
<?php

// Database connection (PDO)
$pdo = new PDO('mysql:host=localhost;dbname=testdb', 'username', 'password');

$pdo->setAttribute(PDO::ATTR_ERRMODE, PDO::ERRMODE_EXCEPTION);

// Check if a file is uploaded
if ($_SERVER['REQUEST_METHOD'] == 'POST' && isset($_FILES['file'])) {

    $uploadDir = 'uploads/'; // Directory to save uploaded files
    $fileName = basename($_FILES['file']['name']); // Get file name

    $filePath = $uploadDir . uniqid() . '-' . $fileName;
    // Above: Create unique file name to avoid overwriting

    // Validate file type and size
    $fileType = pathinfo($fileName, PATHINFO_EXTENSION);
    if ($fileType == 'jpg' || $fileType == 'png') {
        // Move uploaded file to the server
        if (move_uploaded_file($_FILES['file']['tmp_name'], $filePath)) {

            // Prepare SQL statement to insert file path into database
            $stmt = $pdo->prepare("INSERT INTO files (file_name, file_path) VALUES (:file_name, :file_path)");

            $stmt->bindParam(':file_name', $fileName);
            $stmt->bindParam(':file_path', $filePath);
            $stmt->execute();
            echo "File uploaded and path stored successfully!";
        } else {
            echo "Error uploading the file.";
```

```
    }
  } else {
      echo "Invalid file type. Only JPG and PNG allowed.";
  }
}

?>
```

In this PHP example:

The file path is generated with uniqid() to avoid overwriting.

We store the file path in the database using a prepared statement, which protects against SQL injection.

Storing File Paths in Java (Using JDBC)

In Java, you can store file paths in a database similarly by using JDBC (Java Database Connectivity). Here's how you can achieve it:

```java
import java.io.File;
import java.io.FileOutputStream;
import java.io.InputStream;
import java.sql.Connection;
import java.sql.DriverManager;
import java.sql.PreparedStatement;

public class FileUploadExample {
    public static void main(String[] args) {
        String jdbcUrl = "jdbc:mysql://localhost:3306/testdb";
        String username = "root";
        String password = "password";

        try {
```

```java
        // Connect to the database
        Connection conn = DriverManager.getConnection(jdbcUrl,
username, password);

        // Simulate file upload process
        String fileName = "example.png";
        String uploadDir = "uploads/";
        String filePath = uploadDir + System.currentTimeMillis() + "-" +
fileName;

        // Save the file to the local system (simulate file upload)
        File uploadedFile = new File(filePath);

        try (InputStream fileContent = new
FileInputStream("localfile.png");

            FileOutputStream fos = new
FileOutputStream(uploadedFile)) {

                byte[] buffer = new byte[1024];
                int bytesRead;
                while ((bytesRead = fileContent.read(buffer)) != -1) {
                    fos.write(buffer, 0, bytesRead);
                }
            }

        // Prepare SQL statement to store file path
        String sql = "INSERT INTO files (file_name, file_path)
VALUES (?, ?)";

        PreparedStatement stmt = conn.prepareStatement(sql);
        stmt.setString(1, fileName);
        stmt.setString(2, filePath);

        // Execute the query
        stmt.executeUpdate();
        System.out.println("File path stored successfully!");

    } catch (Exception e) {
        e.printStackTrace();
    }
  }
}
```

In this Java example:

We simulate a file upload by writing a file to a directory.

The file path is stored securely in the database using a PreparedStatement to prevent SQL injection.

Handling File Upload Errors in PHP

PHP provides several built-in error codes when dealing with file uploads. Here are some common file upload errors and how to handle them:

```php
<?php
if ($_FILES['file']['error'] == UPLOAD_ERR_OK) {
    // Handle the file upload
} else {
    switch ($_FILES['file']['error']) {
        case UPLOAD_ERR_INI_SIZE:
            echo "The uploaded file exceeds the upload_max_filesize
directive in php.ini.";

            break;
        case UPLOAD_ERR_FORM_SIZE:
            echo "The uploaded file exceeds the MAX_FILE_SIZE
directive in the HTML form.";

            break;
        case UPLOAD_ERR_PARTIAL:
            echo "The file was only partially uploaded.";
            break;
        case UPLOAD_ERR_NO_FILE:
            echo "No file was uploaded.";
            break;
        // Handle other errors...
        default:
            echo "Unknown error occurred.";
            break;
    }
```

```
}
?>
```

In PHP:

UPLOAD_ERR_INI_SIZE, UPLOAD_ERR_FORM_SIZE, and other constants help identify different errors.

A switch block is used to display appropriate error messages.

Handling File Upload Errors in Java

In Java, you can handle file upload errors by catching exceptions related to file I/O or database operations:

```java
try {

    // Simulate file upload process
    String fileName = "example.png";
    File uploadedFile = new File("uploads/" + fileName);

    if (uploadedFile.exists()) {
        throw new IOException("File already exists!");
    }

    // Proceed with file upload logic
    // ...

} catch (IOException e) {
    System.out.println("File upload error: " + e.getMessage());
}
```

In this Java example:

We handle file upload issues like file already existing by throwing an IOException.

We catch exceptions to provide meaningful error messages.

Chapter 10: **Pagination with PDO**

Pagination with PDO is a technique used to divide large sets of data into smaller, more manageable chunks, allowing users to navigate through data efficiently. By using SQL queries along with the LIMIT and OFFSET clauses, you can retrieve a subset of records from the database in each request. PDO enables secure and efficient execution of paginated queries through prepared statements, helping prevent SQL injection. For example, to display 10 records per page, you would calculate the OFFSET based on the current page number and use it in your query. Implementing pagination with PDO involves determining the total number of records, calculating the number of pages needed, and retrieving only the required data for the current page. This method enhances performance, reduces load times, and provides a user-friendly way to browse large data sets.

Why Pagination?

Pagination is crucial for improving performance and user experience when dealing with large datasets. Instead of loading thousands or even millions of records at once, pagination allows the server to fetch smaller, more manageable chunks of data. This reduces memory consumption, speeds up query execution, and ensures faster response times. It also prevents overwhelming users with too much data on a single page and provides an intuitive way to navigate through the data. Without pagination, large datasets could slow down the server, increase load times, and lead to a poor user experience.

Implementing Pagination with PHP and PDO

In PHP, you can implement pagination using PDO by leveraging the LIMIT and OFFSET clauses in your SQL queries. This limits the number of records returned per page and calculates the starting point based on the current page.

Example in PHP

```php
<?php

// Database connection
$pdo = new PDO('mysql:host=localhost;dbname=testdb', 'username', 'password');

// Define the number of results per page
$results_per_page = 10;

// Get the current page number from the URL (default is 1)
$page = isset($_GET['page']) ? (int)$_GET['page'] : 1;

// Calculate the starting point for the records
$offset = ($page - 1) * $results_per_page;
```

```php
// Query to fetch paginated results
$sql = "SELECT * FROM users LIMIT :limit OFFSET :offset";
$stmt = $pdo->prepare($sql);
$stmt->bindValue(':limit', $results_per_page, PDO::PARAM_INT);
$stmt->bindValue(':offset', $offset, PDO::PARAM_INT);
$stmt->execute();

// Fetch and display results
$results = $stmt->fetchAll(PDO::FETCH_ASSOC);
foreach ($results as $row) {
    echo $row['name'] . "<br>";
}

// Determine the total number of records
$total_sql = "SELECT COUNT(*) FROM users";
$total_stmt = $pdo->query($total_sql);
$total_rows = $total_stmt->fetchColumn();

// Calculate total pages
$total_pages = ceil($total_rows / $results_per_page);

// Display pagination links
for ($i = 1; $i <= $total_pages; $i++) {
    echo "<a href='?page=$i'>$i</a> ";
}

?>
```

In this example:

We first establish a PDO connection to the database.

We calculate the offset based on the current page and use the LIMIT and OFFSET SQL clauses to limit the number of rows returned.

After executing the query, we loop through the results and display them.

Finally, we calculate the total number of pages and display pagination links.

Implementing Pagination with Java and JDBC

In Java, you can implement pagination using JDBC by similarly employing SQL's LIMIT and OFFSET clauses to control the number of records returned.

Example in Java

```java
import java.sql.*;

public class PaginationExample {
    public static void main(String[] args) {
        String url = "jdbc:mysql://localhost:3306/testdb";
        String username = "root";
        String password = "password";

        int resultsPerPage = 10;
        int page = 1;
        // Above: Example page number, can be dynamically set
        // based on user input

        try (Connection conn = DriverManager.getConnection(url, username, password)) {

            // Calculate the starting point
```

```java
        int offset = (page - 1) * resultsPerPage;

        // SQL query with LIMIT and OFFSET
        String sql = "SELECT * FROM users LIMIT ? OFFSET ?";
        PreparedStatement stmt = conn.prepareStatement(sql);
        stmt.setInt(1, resultsPerPage);
        stmt.setInt(2, offset);

        // Execute query and process results
        ResultSet rs = stmt.executeQuery();
        while (rs.next()) {
            System.out.println(rs.getString("name"));
        }

        // Query to get total number of records
        String countSql = "SELECT COUNT(*) FROM users";
        Statement countStmt = conn.createStatement();
        ResultSet countRs = countStmt.executeQuery(countSql);
        if (countRs.next()) {
            int totalRows = countRs.getInt(1);

        int totalPages = (int) Math.ceil(totalRows / (double)
resultsPerPage);

            // Display pagination
            for (int i = 1; i <= totalPages; i++) {
                System.out.print(i + " ");
            }
        }

    } catch (SQLException e) {
        e.printStackTrace();
    }
  }
}
```

In this Java example:

We connect to the database using DriverManager.

The SQL query uses LIMIT and OFFSET to paginate the

results.

We retrieve and display the data, and then execute a

separate query to count the total number of records to calculate the total number of pages.

The for loop displays pagination links for each page.

Chapter 11: Using PDO with Multiple Databases

Using PDO with multiple databases allows developers to interact with different database systems within the same application, providing flexibility and scalability. PDO (PHP Data Objects) supports a variety of database drivers, such as MySQL, PostgreSQL, and SQLite, making it easy to connect and execute queries on multiple databases simultaneously. To manage multiple connections, you can create separate PDO instances for each database, specifying the appropriate DSN (Data Source Name) for each connection. By utilizing PDO's abstraction layer, switching between databases or performing operations across different databases becomes more streamlined.

For example, a single application could read from a MySQL database and write to a PostgreSQL database using different PDO objects, all while maintaining consistent error handling and query execution methods. This feature is particularly useful for applications that need to migrate data between systems or run analytics across multiple databases.

Switching to Other Databases with PDO

PDO in PHP and Java provides a flexible way to connect to

different databases such as MySQL, PostgreSQL, SQLite, and more. By adjusting the connection string, developers can easily switch between databases without altering the query logic, provided the SQL syntax is compatible.

PHP Example

In PHP, PDO supports multiple database systems by specifying the Data Source Name (DSN) in the connection string. Here's how to connect to different databases:

```
// MySQL connection
$mysqlPDO = new PDO('mysql:host=localhost;dbname=testdb',
'username', 'password');

// PostgreSQL connection
$pgsqlPDO = new PDO('pgsql:host=localhost;dbname=testdb',
'username', 'password');

// SQLite connection
$sqlitePDO = new PDO('sqlite:/path/to/database.db');

// Set error mode to exception
$mysqlPDO->setAttribute(PDO::ATTR_ERRMODE,
PDO::ERRMODE_EXCEPTION);

$pgsqlPDO->setAttribute(PDO::ATTR_ERRMODE,
PDO::ERRMODE_EXCEPTION);

$sqlitePDO->setAttribute(PDO::ATTR_ERRMODE,
PDO::ERRMODE_EXCEPTION);
```

In the example above, you can see that each database type requires a different DSN format (mysql, pgsql, and sqlite), but the method for interacting with the databases remains consistent.

Java Example

In Java, the approach is similar, using JDBC to interact with different databases by specifying the correct JDBC URL for each database type. Here's an example of how to connect to MySQL, PostgreSQL, and SQLite using JDBC:

```
// MySQL connection
Connection mysqlConnection =
DriverManager.getConnection("jdbc:mysql://localhost:3306/testdb",
"username", "password");

// PostgreSQL connection
Connection pgsqlConnection =
DriverManager.getConnection("jdbc:postgresql://localhost:5432/testdb
", "username", "password");

// SQLite connection
Connection sqliteConnection =
DriverManager.getConnection("jdbc:sqlite:/path/to/database.db");
```

The URL format for each database differs: MySQL uses jdbc:mysql://, PostgreSQL uses jdbc:postgresql://, and SQLite uses jdbc:sqlite://.

Handling SQL Syntax Differences

When switching between databases, it's essential to consider the differences in SQL syntax, as each database system may have slightly different rules or features.

Example 1: LIMIT vs TOP

In MySQL and PostgreSQL, to limit the number of rows returned, you use LIMIT. However, in SQL Server, the equivalent would be TOP.

MySQL/PostgreSQL Syntax:

SELECT * FROM users LIMIT 10;

SQL Server Syntax:

SELECT TOP 10 * FROM users;

Example 2: AUTO_INCREMENT vs SERIAL

In MySQL, the auto-incrementing of primary keys is done using AUTO_INCREMENT, while in PostgreSQL, it uses SERIAL or a sequence.

MySQL Syntax:

```
CREATE TABLE users (
    id INT AUTO_INCREMENT PRIMARY KEY,
    name VARCHAR(255)
);
```

PostgreSQL Syntax:

```sql
CREATE TABLE users (
    id SERIAL PRIMARY KEY,
    name VARCHAR(255)
);
```

By understanding these differences and using PDO (in PHP) or JDBC (in Java), developers can seamlessly switch between databases and handle queries that might need to be adapted for different SQL dialects. For complex applications, abstraction layers or ORM frameworks can also help manage these differences and maintain a consistent interface.

Chapter 12: Building a Simple Application with PDO

Build a simple User Registration App using MySQL and PHP PDO

This chapter shows you how to build a simple user registration application using PHP and MySQL with PDO. This application will allow users to register by providing their name, email, and password, and the data will be securely stored in a MySQL database.

Prerequisites:

PHP 7 or higher

MySQL server

Basic knowledge of PHP and SQL

PDO extension enabled in PHP (it's enabled by default in most PHP installations)

Set up the MySQL database

First, create a database and a users table to store the user's information.

```sql
CREATE DATABASE user_registration;

USE user_registration;

CREATE TABLE users (
    id INT AUTO_INCREMENT PRIMARY KEY,
    name VARCHAR(255) NOT NULL,
    email VARCHAR(255) UNIQUE NOT NULL,
    password VARCHAR(255) NOT NULL
);
```

Create the registration form (HTML)

The form will allow users to enter their name, email, and password. We'll make sure the form uses the POST method to send data to a PHP script.

```html
<!DOCTYPE html>
<html lang="en">
<head>
    <meta charset="UTF-8">
    <meta name="viewport" content="width=device-width, initial-scale=1.0">
    <title>User Registration</title>
</head>
<body>
```

```html
<h2>User Registration</h2>
<form action="register.php" method="post">
    <label for="name">Name:</label>
    <input type="text" id="name" name="name" required><br><br>

    <label for="email">Email:</label>
    <input type="email" id="email" name="email" required><br><br>

    <label for="password">Password:</label>
    <input type="password" id="password" name="password" required><br><br>

    <button type="submit">Register</button>
    </form>
</body>
</html>
```

Set up PDO database connection (db.php)

This script will handle the connection to the MySQL database using PDO.

```php
<?php

$host = 'localhost'; // Database host
$dbname = 'user_registration'; // Database name
$username = 'root'; // Your MySQL username
$password = ''; // Your MySQL password

try {
    // Create a PDO instance
    $pdo = new PDO("mysql:host=$host;dbname=$dbname", $username, $password);

    // Set the PDO error mode to exception
```

```php
    $pdo->setAttribute(PDO::ATTR_ERRMODE,
PDO::ERRMODE_EXCEPTION);

} catch (PDOException $e) {
    // If an error occurs, display a message
    echo 'Connection failed: ' . $e->getMessage();
}

?>
```

Handle the registration process (register.php)

This script will handle the user registration logic. It will validate the input, hash the password for security, and store the user's data in the database.

```php
<?php

// Include the database connection
include('db.php');

// Check if the form is submitted
if ($_SERVER['REQUEST_METHOD'] == 'POST') {
    // Collect user data from the form
    $name = $_POST['name'];
    $email = $_POST['email'];
    $password = $_POST['password'];

    // Validate email format
    if (!filter_var($email, FILTER_VALIDATE_EMAIL)) {
        echo "Invalid email format.";
        exit;
    }

    // Hash the password using password_hash
```

```php
    $hashedPassword = password_hash($password,
PASSWORD_DEFAULT);

    // Prepare an SQL statement to insert user data
    $sql = "INSERT INTO users (name, email, password) VALUES
(:name, :email, :password)";

    $stmt = $pdo->prepare($sql);

    // Bind parameters
    $stmt->bindParam(':name', $name);
    $stmt->bindParam(':email', $email);
    $stmt->bindParam(':password', $hashedPassword);

    try {
        // Execute the statement to insert the data into the database
        $stmt->execute();
        echo "Registration successful! <a href='login.php'>Login
here</a>";

    } catch (PDOException $e) {
        // If an error occurs, display an error message
        echo "Error: " . $e->getMessage();
    }
}

?>
```

Test the registration

Make sure your web server is running (e.g., Apache or Nginx).

Open the registration form (index.html or similar) in a web

browser.

Fill out the form and submit it.

The data should be inserted into the users table in the database, and you'll see the "Registration successful!" message.

Security considerations:

Password hashing: The password is hashed before being stored in the database using password_hash(), which is a strong and secure hashing function.

Prepared statements: Using prepared statements with bound parameters (like :name, :email, and :password) ensures protection against SQL injection attacks.

Optional: Add login functionality

If you want to add a login page, you can create a login.php page where users can enter their credentials to log in.

```php
<?php

include('db.php');

if ($_SERVER['REQUEST_METHOD'] == 'POST') {
    $email = $_POST['email'];
    $password = $_POST['password'];

    // Prepare the SQL query to fetch user data
    $sql = "SELECT * FROM users WHERE email = :email";
    $stmt = $pdo->prepare($sql);

    $stmt->bindParam(':email', $email);

    $stmt->execute();
    $user = $stmt->fetch(PDO::FETCH_ASSOC);

    if ($user && password_verify($password, $user['password'])) {
        echo "Login successful! Welcome, " . $user['name'];
    } else {
        echo "Invalid email or password.";
    }
}
?>
<form action="login.php" method="post">
    <label for="email">Email:</label>
    <input type="email" id="email" name="email" required><br><br>

    <label for="password">Password:</label>
    <input type="password" id="password" name="password"
required><br><br>

    <button type="submit">Login</button>
</form>
```

This simple user registration app demonstrates how to use PHP and MySQL with PDO for securely handling user registration and login processes. The app hashes passwords for security, validates user input, and uses prepared statements to protect against SQL injection.

You can further enhance this app by adding features like email verification, password reset, or user profile management.

Build a simple User Registration App using MySQL and Java PDO

Build a simple user registration application using Java and MySQL with JDBC (Java Database Connectivity). This application will allow users to register by providing their name, email, and password, and the data will be securely stored in a MySQL database.

Prerequisites:

Java Development Kit (JDK) installed on your machine.

MySQL server.

Basic knowledge of Java, JDBC, and SQL.

MySQL JDBC driver (downloadable from the MySQL website).

Set up the MySQL Database

First, create a MySQL database and a users table to store the user's information.

```
CREATE DATABASE user_registration;

USE user_registration;

CREATE TABLE users (
    id INT AUTO_INCREMENT PRIMARY KEY,
    name VARCHAR(255) NOT NULL,
    email VARCHAR(255) UNIQUE NOT NULL,
    password VARCHAR(255) NOT NULL
);
```

Add MySQL JDBC Driver to Your Java Project

To connect to MySQL, you need the MySQL JDBC driver (mysql-connector-java). You can download it from the MySQL Connector/J website, or if you're using Maven, you can add the dependency:

```
<dependency>
    <groupId>mysql</groupId>
    <artifactId>mysql-connector-java</artifactId>
    <version>8.0.29</version>
</dependency>
```

Create the User Registration Form (HTML)

This form allows users to enter their name, email, and password.

```
<!DOCTYPE html>
<html lang="en">
<head>
   <meta charset="UTF-8">
   <meta name="viewport" content="width=device-width,
initial-scale=1.0">

   <title>User Registration</title>
</head>
<body>
   <h2>User Registration</h2>
   <form action="register" method="post">
     <label for="name">Name:</label>
     <input type="text" id="name" name="name" required><br><br>

     <label for="email">Email:</label>
     <input type="email" id="email" name="email" required><br><br>

     <label for="password">Password:</label>
     <input type="password" id="password" name="password"
required><br><br>

     <button type="submit">Register</button>
   </form>
</body>
</html>
```

Set up the Database Connection (DB.java)

This class will handle the connection to the MySQL database using JDBC.

```java
import java.sql.Connection;
import java.sql.DriverManager;
import java.sql.SQLException;

public class DB {
    private static final String URL =
"jdbc:mysql://localhost:3306/user_registration";
    private static final String USER = "root"; // MySQL username
    private static final String PASSWORD = ""; // MySQL password

    public static Connection getConnection() throws SQLException {
        try {
            // Load and register the JDBC driver (if necessary, for older
            // Java versions)
            Class.forName("com.mysql.cj.jdbc.Driver");

            // Connect to the MySQL database
            return DriverManager.getConnection(URL, USER,
PASSWORD);

        } catch (ClassNotFoundException e) {
            throw new SQLException("MySQL JDBC Driver not found.",
e);

        }
    }
}
```

Handle the User Registration Logic (RegisterServlet.java)

This servlet will process the form submission. It validates the email, hashes the password, and stores the data in the database.

```java
import java.io.*;
import javax.servlet.*;
import javax.servlet.http.*;
import java.sql.*;

public class RegisterServlet extends HttpServlet {

    @Override
    protected void doPost(HttpServletRequest request,
HttpServletResponse response) throws ServletException,
IOException {

        // Retrieve form data
        String name = request.getParameter("name");
        String email = request.getParameter("email");
        String password = request.getParameter("password");

        // Validate email format
        if (!email.contains("@")) {
            response.getWriter().println("Invalid email format.");
            return;
        }

        // Hash the password for security
        String hashedPassword = BCrypt.hashpw(password,
BCrypt.gensalt());

        // Insert the data into the database
        try (Connection conn = DB.getConnection()) {
            String sql = "INSERT INTO users (name, email, password)
VALUES (?, ?, ?)";
```

```java
        try (PreparedStatement stmt = conn.prepareStatement(sql)) {
            stmt.setString(1, name);
            stmt.setString(2, email);
            stmt.setString(3, hashedPassword);

            int result = stmt.executeUpdate();
            if (result > 0) {
                response.getWriter().println("Registration successful! <a
href='login.html'>Login here</a>");

            } else {
                response.getWriter().println("Registration failed.");
            }
        }
    } catch (SQLException e) {
        e.printStackTrace();
        response.getWriter().println("Database error: " +
e.getMessage());
    }
  }
}
```

In this example:

We use BCrypt (from the jBCrypt library) to hash the password before storing it. You can add the dependency for jBCrypt using Maven:

```xml
<dependency>
  <groupId>org.mindrot</groupId>
  <artifactId>jbcrypt</artifactId>
  <version>0.4</version>
</dependency>
```

Set Up web.xml to Map the Servlet (web.xml)

In a Java web application (Servlet-based), you need to map your servlet to a URL in the web.xml configuration file.

```xml
<web-app xmlns="http://java.sun.com/xml/ns/javaee"
xmlns:xsi="http://www.w3.org/2001/XMLSchema-instance"

xsi:schemaLocation="http://java.sun.com/xml/ns/javaee
http://java.sun.com/xml/ns/javaee/web-app_3_0.xsd"
version="3.0">

<servlet>
<servlet-name>RegisterServlet</servlet-name>
<servlet-class>RegisterServlet</servlet-class>
</servlet>
<servlet-mapping>
<url-pattern>/register</url-pattern>
</servlet-mapping>
</web-app>
```

Compile your code

Create a Dynamic Web Project in Eclipse (or your IDE of choice)

If you're using an IDE like Eclipse, you can follow these steps:

Open Eclipse and create a new Dynamic Web Project.

Go to **File > New > Dynamic Web Project**.

Name it, for example, UserRegistrationApp.

Choose a target runtime (e.g., Apache Tomcat).

Click Finish.

Set Up Project Structure

Inside the WebContent directory, create a structure like this:

UserRegistrationApp

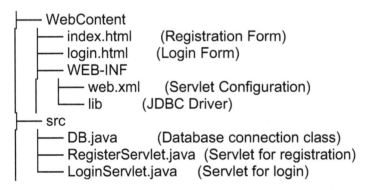

```
├── WebContent
│   ├── index.html      (Registration Form)
│   ├── login.html      (Login Form)
│   ├── WEB-INF
│   │   ├── web.xml      (Servlet Configuration)
│   │   └── lib          (JDBC Driver)
├── src
│   ├── DB.java          (Database connection class)
│   ├── RegisterServlet.java  (Servlet for registration)
│   └── LoginServlet.java     (Servlet for login)
```

index.html: The registration form

web.xml: The servlet configuration

WEB-INF/lib/: The directory where you will place the MySQL JDBC driver (mysql-connector-java-x.x.x.jar)

Add the MySQL JDBC Driver to the Project

Download the MySQL JDBC driver (e.g., mysql-connector-java-x.x.x.jar) from the official MySQL site, and place it in the WEB-INF/lib/ directory of your project.

In Eclipse, you can also add the MySQL JDBC JAR to your project by right-clicking on your project > Build Path > Configure Build Path, then adding the JAR file.

Configure web.xml

Make sure your web.xml (inside WEB-INF/) maps the RegisterServlet and LoginServlet:


```
<web-app xmlns="http://java.sun.com/xml/ns/javaee"
xmlns:xsi="http://www.w3.org/2001/XMLSchema-instance"
xsi:schemaLocation="http://java.sun.com/xml/ns/javaee
http://java.sun.com/xml/ns/javaee/web-app_3_0.xsd" version="3.0">
<servlet>
<servlet-name>RegisterServlet</servlet-name>
<servlet-class>RegisterServlet</servlet-class>
</servlet>
<servlet-mapping>
<url-pattern>/register</url-pattern>
</servlet-mapping>
<servlet>
<servlet-name>LoginServlet</servlet-name>
<servlet-class>LoginServlet</servlet-class>
</servlet>
```

```
<servlet-mapping>
<url-pattern>/login</url-pattern>
</servlet-mapping>
</web-app>
```

Compile Java Code

To compile Java code in Eclipse, follow these steps:

In Eclipse:

Right-click on your project.

Select Build Project.

If you're not using an IDE and compiling via the command line, you would need to compile Java files using the javac command.

Assuming you have the DB.java, RegisterServlet.java, and LoginServlet.java files saved in a directory structure, run the following command in the terminal:

```
javac -cp .:path/to/mysql-connector-java-x.x.x.jar -d WEB-INF/classes src/*.java
```

Here, replace path/to/mysql-connector-java-x.x.x.jar with the actual path to the MySQL JDBC driver. The -d WEB-

INF/classes specifies the output directory for compiled files.

Deploy the Application to Apache Tomcat

To deploy the application to Apache Tomcat:

Start Tomcat: Ensure your Tomcat server is up and running.

Deploy: Copy the UserRegistrationApp.war file (or simply copy the entire project folder if you're using an IDE like Eclipse) to the webapps/ directory in your Tomcat installation.

If you're using Eclipse, you can deploy the app directly by right-clicking the project and selecting Run on Server (assuming you've configured Apache Tomcat in Eclipse).

If you're using the command line, you can manually copy the WAR file (created from your project) to the webapps/ folder of Tomcat and start the Tomcat server.

Access the Registration Form

Once Tomcat is running, navigate to the following URL in your web browser:

http://localhost:8080/UserRegistrationApp/

This will load the index.html page, and you should be able to fill out the registration form. Upon submission, the data will be saved to your MySQL database.

Test the Registration

Make sure your web server (e.g., Apache Tomcat) is running.

Deploy your application to the server.

Open the registration form (index.html) in a web browser.

Fill out the form and submit it.

The data should be inserted into the users table in the database, and you'll see the "Registration successful!" message.

Security Considerations:

Password hashing: The password is hashed before being stored in the database using BCrypt, which is a strong and secure hashing algorithm.

Prepared statements: Using prepared statements with parameterized queries (?) prevents SQL injection attacks.

Optional: Add Login Functionality

To add a login page, create a LoginServlet.java that checks if the entered email and password match the values stored in the database.

```
import java.io.*;
import javax.servlet.*;
import javax.servlet.http.*;
import java.sql.*;

public class LoginServlet extends HttpServlet {

    @Override
    protected void doPost(HttpServletRequest request,
HttpServletResponse response) throws ServletException,
IOException {

        String email = request.getParameter("email");
```

```java
String password = request.getParameter("password");

try (Connection conn = DB.getConnection()) {
    String sql = "SELECT * FROM users WHERE email = ?";
    try (PreparedStatement stmt = conn.prepareStatement(sql)) {
        stmt.setString(1, email);

        ResultSet rs = stmt.executeQuery();
        if (rs.next()) {
            String storedPassword = rs.getString("password");
            if (BCrypt.checkpw(password, storedPassword)) {
                response.getWriter().println("Login successful!
Welcome, " + rs.getString("name"));

            } else {
                response.getWriter().println("Invalid password.");
            }
        } else {
            response.getWriter().println("Email not found.");
        }
    }
} catch (SQLException e) {
    e.printStackTrace();
    response.getWriter().println("Database error: " +
e.getMessage());
    }
  }
}
```

This simple user registration app demonstrates how to use Java and MySQL with JDBC for securely handling user registration and login processes. The app hashes passwords for security, validates user input, and uses prepared statements to protect against SQL injection.

You can further enhance this app by adding features like email verification, password reset, or user profile management.

Appendices

Appendix A: Further Learning: Suggested resources for mastering MySQL

Mastering MySQL involves gaining a deep understanding of its architecture, query optimization, advanced SQL techniques, and database administration. Below are some excellent resources to further your MySQL knowledge and enhance your skills.

Books

"MySQL: The Complete Reference" by Vikram Vaswani

This book offers comprehensive coverage of MySQL's features, from basic queries to advanced techniques like replication and clustering. It's perfect for both beginners and seasoned professionals.

"High Performance MySQL" by Baron Schwartz, Peter Zaitsev, and Vadim Tkachenko

A must-read for anyone serious about MySQL performance tuning. It covers topics like indexing, query optimization, and managing large-scale MySQL databases.

"MySQL Cookbook" by Paul DuBois

This practical guide offers more than 200 MySQL solutions for everyday problems, from data manipulation to advanced database administration.

Online Courses and Tutorials

MySQL Documentation

The official MySQL documentation is a great starting point for anyone looking to learn the ins and outs of MySQL. It's constantly updated and covers everything from installation to advanced configurations.

MySQL Documentation

Udemy: "MySQL for Data Analysis"

A beginner-friendly course that focuses on using MySQL for data analysis, covering essential SQL commands and how to work with databases for analysis and reporting.

MySQL for Data Analysis on Udemy

Coursera: "Databases and SQL for Data Science with Python"

Offered by IBM, this course teaches MySQL basics with hands-on assignments and an introduction to database management systems (DBMS) using SQL.

Databases and SQL for Data Science

Codecademy: "Learn SQL"

Codecademy offers interactive SQL courses that include practice problems and real-world exercises to help you gain proficiency with databases like MySQL.

Learn SQL on Codecademy

Forums and Communities

Stack Overflow

Stack Overflow has a large community of MySQL users where you can find solutions to common (and uncommon) problems. Participate in discussions or ask questions to get personalized help.

MySQL on Stack Overflow

MySQL Forums

The official MySQL forums are a valuable resource for troubleshooting and learning from experienced database administrators and developers.

MySQL Community Forums

Reddit: r/mysql

A community on Reddit where MySQL enthusiasts share articles, tutorials, and experiences. Great for discovering best practices and real-world use cases.

r/mysql on Reddit

Blogs and Articles

Percona Blog

Percona is a leading company in MySQL support and offers an excellent blog with tips, tutorials, and optimization techniques to improve your MySQL skills.

MySQL Performance Blog by Peter Zaitsev

Written by the author of "High Performance MySQL," this blog is filled with insights on optimizing and tuning MySQL databases, with a focus on large-scale operations.

MySQL Performance Blog

Several Nines Blog

Several Nines is known for providing high availability and automation tools for MySQL and other databases. Their blog offers great content on MySQL clustering, replication, and scaling.

YouTube Channels

MySQL Official Channel

The official MySQL YouTube channel offers webinars, conference talks, and tutorials on various aspects of MySQL, including advanced topics.

MySQL Official YouTube Channel

Tech with Tim

Tech with Tim is a great YouTube channel for beginners and intermediate learners that provides tutorials on MySQL and programming languages, with a focus on real-world projects.

Advanced Learning: Performance and Scaling

"MySQL Performance Tuning" by Brendan Gregg

Focused on performance, this book teaches techniques for

improving MySQL performance, understanding the underlying architecture, and debugging slow queries.

"Mastering MySQL" by Korry Douglas

This book goes deeper into complex MySQL topics, covering advanced performance techniques, replication, and high-availability clustering.

Certification

MySQL Database Administrator (CMDBA) Certification

Oracle offers the MySQL Certified Database Administrator (CMDBA) certification. This certification is ideal for database administrators who want to validate their skills and experience.

Appendix B: Further Learning: Suggested resources for mastering PHP

Mastering PHP involves learning not just the syntax but also understanding best practices, security, performance optimization, and advanced concepts such as object-oriented programming (OOP) and frameworks. Below are suggested resources that will help deepen your PHP knowledge, whether you're a beginner or a seasoned developer.

Books

"PHP & MySQL: Novice to Ninja" by Tom Butler

A comprehensive guide for beginners to advanced users, this book teaches PHP in the context of MySQL databases. It covers topics such as user authentication, security, and dynamic web applications.

"Modern PHP: New Features and Good Practices" by Josh Lockhart

This book focuses on best practices, object-oriented programming, and how to modernize your PHP code. It also includes advanced concepts such as dependency injection and service containers.

"PHP Objects, Patterns, and Practice" by Mika Schwartz

A great resource for PHP developers who want to dive into object-oriented programming and design patterns. It covers real-world applications, testing, and common design patterns used in PHP.

Online Courses and Tutorials

PHP Manual

The official PHP manual is an invaluable resource for learning the language's syntax and functions. It includes thorough documentation, examples, and references for all built-in PHP functions.

Udemy: "PHP for Beginners"

This beginner-friendly course on Udemy teaches the basics of PHP, from setting up a PHP development environment to working with variables, arrays, and forms.

LinkedIn Learning: "PHP Essential Training"

A highly rated course by Kevin Skoglund on LinkedIn Learning that covers everything from the basics of PHP to handling forms, sending emails, and working with databases.

Codecademy: "Learn PHP"

An interactive learning platform with hands-on exercises that guide you through the basics of PHP programming.

Frameworks and Tools

Laravel Documentation

Laravel is one of the most popular PHP frameworks. Its elegant syntax and robust features make it a go-to choice for modern PHP development. The official documentation provides everything from installation to advanced use cases.

Symfony Documentation

Symfony is another powerful PHP framework that focuses on reusable components and scalability. The official Symfony documentation covers setup, components, and advanced configurations for building enterprise-level applications.

CodeIgniter Documentation

A lightweight PHP framework ideal for building small to medium applications quickly. Its documentation is beginner-friendly and covers all the essentials for working with the framework.

Forums and Communities

Stack Overflow

Stack Overflow hosts an active community of PHP developers who share solutions, answer questions, and discuss best practices. It's an essential resource for troubleshooting and getting expert advice.

PHP Reddit Community (r/php)

A vibrant community on Reddit where you can engage with fellow PHP developers, share articles, and ask for advice on everything from basic queries to complex problems.

PHP Freaks Forum

A dedicated forum for PHP developers that includes tutorials, code samples, and a large community of experienced developers to help with any PHP-related issues.

Blogs and Articles

PHP: The Right Way

A community-driven initiative that provides a comprehensive guide to best practices in PHP development. It covers everything from coding standards to security practices.

Tuts+ PHP Tutorials

Tuts+ offers in-depth tutorials for both beginners and advanced PHP developers. Topics include working with APIs, building applications, and using PHP frameworks.

SitePoint PHP Blog

SitePoint offers a variety of high-quality tutorials, articles, and resources on PHP development. From performance tips to security practices, it's a go-to source for web developers.

YouTube Channels

PHP Official Channel

The official PHP channel provides webinars, conference talks, and tutorials on all aspects of PHP, including new features, best practices, and practical advice.

Traversy Media

Traversy Media offers fantastic tutorials and crash courses for PHP and web development. His PHP tutorials cover everything from basics to full-fledged projects using modern PHP techniques.

Codecourse

Codecourse is a YouTube channel with tutorials for PHP developers, focusing on building projects with frameworks like Laravel and practical coding examples.

Advanced Learning: Design Patterns and Best Practices

"PHP Objects, Patterns, and Practice" by Mika Schwartz

For developers who want to dive deeper into object-oriented design and design patterns, this book explores best practices and real-world applications.

"Design Patterns in PHP and Laravel" by Arda Kadir Duman

This book teaches design patterns in PHP, specifically within the Laravel framework. It's a great resource for developers who want to architect scalable and maintainable applications.

Certification

Zend Certified PHP Engineer (ZCE)

The Zend certification is one of the most recognized certifications for PHP professionals. It validates your skills and knowledge in PHP development, including core PHP functions and object-oriented programming.

Appendix C: Further Learning: Suggested resources for mastering Java

Mastering Java involves a strong understanding of core programming concepts, object-oriented design, libraries, frameworks, and tools. Whether you are a beginner or an advanced developer, the following resources will help you deepen your knowledge and skills in Java development.

Books

"Effective Java" by Joshua Bloch

One of the most respected books for Java developers, it focuses on best practices, coding techniques, and design patterns. It covers topics like generics, concurrency, and the effective use of Java APIs.

"Java: The Complete Reference" by Herbert Schildt

This is a comprehensive guide to the Java programming language. It serves as both a beginner's guide and a reference book, covering everything from basic syntax to advanced features like Java 8's lambdas and streams.

"Head First Java" by Kathy Sierra and Bert Bates

A beginner-friendly book that explains Java concepts through engaging visuals and real-world examples. It's excellent for those just starting with Java programming.

"Java Concurrency in Practice" by Brian Goetz

This book is for Java developers who want to master multi-threading and concurrent programming. It covers synchronization, thread safety, and how to write efficient, scalable Java applications.

Online Courses and Tutorials

Oracle Java Tutorials

Oracle, the official steward of Java, provides free and comprehensive tutorials covering everything from basic syntax to advanced topics like concurrency and GUI programming.

Udemy: "Java Programming Masterclass for Software Developers"

This is one of the best-rated courses on Udemy, teaching Java from the ground up. It covers core concepts, object-oriented programming, data structures, algorithms, and introduces you to Java frameworks like Spring.

Coursera: "Java Programming and Software Engineering Fundamentals"

A beginner-friendly series of courses from Duke University on Coursera, which covers the basics of Java programming, problem-solving, data structures, and algorithms.

Codecademy: "Learn Java"

Codecademy offers a hands-on approach to learning Java with interactive lessons that cover the basics and go up to more complex topics like file I/O, collections, and OOP.

Java Frameworks and Tools

Spring Framework Documentation

Spring is one of the most popular Java frameworks for building scalable, enterprise-level applications. The official Spring documentation covers everything from configuration and dependency injection to web development with Spring MVC and building microservices with Spring Boot.

Hibernate Documentation

Hibernate is an ORM (Object-Relational Mapping) tool for Java, and it simplifies database interaction. Its documentation helps developers understand how to integrate it with Java applications, manage sessions, and work with JPA (Java Persistence API).

Maven Documentation

Maven is a build automation tool used for Java projects. Its documentation covers project configuration, dependency management, and how to build, test, and deploy Java applications.

Forums and Communities

Stack Overflow

Stack Overflow is a go-to place for Java developers to ask questions, get answers, and find solutions to common programming challenges. With thousands of Java-related questions and answers, it's an essential resource for troubleshooting.

Reddit: r/java

A vibrant Java community where developers share articles, news, and answer technical questions. It's also a good place to get recommendations on the latest Java trends and frameworks.

Java Forums

Java Forums is a dedicated community for Java developers, including discussions on Java topics, code samples, and job opportunities.

Blogs and Articles

Baeldung

Baeldung offers tutorials and in-depth articles on Java, Spring, Hibernate, and other Java technologies. The content is comprehensive and great for developers looking to learn new libraries, tools, and best practices.

JavaWorld

JavaWorld publishes articles, tutorials, and news about Java technologies, including Java-related libraries, performance, and security practices.

Vlad Mihalcea's Blog

Vlad Mihalcea is an expert in Hibernate and JPA, and his blog is a great resource for learning about performance tuning, best practices in database interaction, and advanced Hibernate techniques.

YouTube Channels

Programming with Mosh

Mosh Hamedani's YouTube channel is an excellent resource for Java developers. He covers a wide range of programming topics, including tutorials on Java basics, OOP, and advanced frameworks.

Java Brains

Java Brains is a channel that focuses on Java tutorials, Java EE, and various Java technologies. It's especially useful for developers looking to dive deeper into frameworks like Spring and Java EE.

Telusko

Telusko's YouTube channel offers Java tutorials for both beginners and advanced developers. The tutorials are clear and concise, and they cover a wide variety of topics, including data structures, algorithms, and Java frameworks.

Advanced Learning: Design Patterns and Best Practices

"Design Patterns: Elements of Reusable Object-Oriented Software" by Erich Gamma, Richard Helm, Ralph Johnson, John Vlissides

While not Java-specific, this book is a must-read for any object-oriented programmer. It introduces design patterns such as Singleton, Factory, and Observer, which are widely used in Java development.

"Java Design Patterns" by Vaskaran Sarcar

This book covers the most common design patterns used in Java programming. It provides practical examples and solutions to software design problems.

"Clean Code: A Handbook of Agile Software Craftsmanship" by Robert C. Martin

Clean Code is an essential book for any software developer. It offers best practices for writing maintainable, readable, and scalable Java code.

Certification

Oracle Certified Professional, Java SE Programmer (OCPJP)

Oracle offers the OCPJP certification, which validates your Java programming skills and understanding of Java's core features. It's widely recognized and adds credibility to your skill set.

Java Developer Certification by Spring Framework

The Spring framework offers certifications for Java developers specializing in building web applications. It's a valuable credential for developers who work with Spring and want to demonstrate their proficiency in enterprise-level Java programming.

www.ingramcontent.com/pod-product-compliance
Lightning Source LLC
LaVergne TN
LVHW022343060326
832902LV00022B/4216